AWAKEN

52 WEEKS OF MINDFUL SPIRITUAL PRACTICE

ADAM R. BOGGESS

Copyright © 2025 by Tatted Chaps Press, LLC

All rights reserved. No part of this publication may be reproduced, stored in a retrieval system, or transmitted in any form or by any means—electronic, mechanical, photocopying, recording, or otherwise—without prior written permission of the author, except in the case of brief quotations used in critical articles or reviews.

Published by Tatted Chaps Press, LLC

www.tattedchapspress.com

ISBN: 979-8-9995220-3-0

❦ Formatted with Vellum

To Kumi and Sena—
You never gave up on me,
even when I thought you should have.
Even in the silence,
even in the shadows,
your love remained steady.
You are the light that kept me reaching for more.

CONTENTS

A Personal Invitation   ix

1. The Grounding Breath (Inspired by Zen Buddhism)   1
2. The Centering Prayer (Inspired by Christian Mysticism)   8
3. Walking Meditation (Inspired by Theravada Buddhism)   15
4. The Gratitude Jar (Inspired by Religion and Social Psychology)   22
5. Body Scan Awareness (Inspired by Vipassana Meditation)   29
6. Loving-Kindness Meditation (Inspired by Metta, Buddhist)   36
7. Sacred Listening (Inspired by Quaker Tradition)   43
8. Nature as Sanctuary (Inspired by Celtic Spirituality)   50
9. The Morning Offering (Inspired by Hinduism)   57
10. Daily Resets (Inspired by Stoicism)   64
11. Chanting (Inspired by Hindu/Bhakti Tradition)   71
12. Sacred Movement (Inspired by Sufism / Whirling Dervishes)   78
13. Sacred Fire Ritual (Inspired by Native American Traditions)   85
14. Silence Retreat (Inspired by Christian Desert Fathers)   92
15. Blessing Food (Inspired by Judaism)   99
16. The Four Directions (Inspired by Indigenous North America)   106
17. Tea Ceremony (Inspired by Japanese Zen)   113
18. Sunrise Renewal (Inspired by Pagan and Neo-Pagan Traditions)   120
19. The Rosary (Inspired by Catholic Christianity)   127
20. Dream Journaling (Inspired by Greek Philosophy / Asclepian Tradition)   134
21. Candle Gazing (Inspired by Trataka, Yoga)   141
22. Sacred Storytelling (Inspired by West African Griot Tradition)   148
23. Mindful Touch (Inspired by Taoist Qi Gong)   154

24. Acts of Service (Inspired by Christianity/Sikhism)   161
25. Labyrinth Walking (Inspired by Christian Mysticism/
    Pagan Europe)   168
26. Fasting (Inspired by Islam and Multiple Traditions)   175
27. Forest Bathing (Inspired by Shinrin-Yoku, Japan)   182
28. Breath of Fire (Inspired by Kundalini Yoga)   189
29. Sacred Geometry (Inspired by Platonic Philosophy/
    Egyptian Temples)   196
30. Purification with Water (Inspired by Shinto Tradition)   203
31. Visualization (Inspired by Tibetan Buddhism)   209
32. Breath Counting (Inspired by Zen Buddhism)   215
33. Naming the Inner Critic (Inspired by Jungian
    Psychology)   221
34. Intention Setting (Inspired by Sankalpa, Yoga Nidra)   228
35. Mantra Meditation (Inspired by Hinduism/ Vedanta)   234
36. Kintsugi (Inspired by Japanese Philosophy)   240
37. Planting as Prayer (Inspired by Indigenous, Agrarian,
    and Earth-Based Traditions)   246
38. Sound Bathing (Inspired by Tibetan Bowls and Global
    Traditions)   253
39. Sacred Weeping (Inspired by Jewish, Sufi, and
    Indigenous Traditions)   260
40. Sacred Offering (Inspired by the Shinto tradition of
    Osaisen)   267
41. Mindful Eating (Inspired by Buddhist and Ayurvedic
    Traditions)   275
42. Fire Gazing (Inspired by Zoroastrian and Indigenous
    Shamanic Traditions)   283
43. Listening to the Land (Inspired by the Cherokee
    Tradition)   290
44. The Quiet Hour (Inspired by Amish Contemplative
    Living)   298
45. Morning Offering (Inspired by the Blackfoot
    Tradition)   306
46. Gazing at the Stars (Inspired by Indigenous, Taoist,
    and Stoic Traditions)   314
47. Compassion Letter (Inspired by Buddhist and
    Psychological Practices)   322
48. Spiritual Bathing (Inspired by Yoruba, Jewish, and
    Indigenous Traditions)   329
49. Practice of Stillness (Inspired by the Yogic Tradition)   336

50. Seasonal Gratitude Offering (Inspired by the Kalasha
    People of the Hindu Kush)   343
51. Remembering the Ancestors (Inspired by Japanese
    Shinto and Buddhist Traditions)   350
52. Building Your Own Ritual (Inspired by the Global
    Tapestry of Practice)   357

Conclusion: Awaken Again—and Keep Becoming   365
Acknowledgments   367
About the Author   369

A PERSONAL INVITATION

Awaken is a 52-week devotional journey intentionally crafted for the spiritually curious, the weary seeker, and the quietly courageous soul. Whether you consider yourself religious, spiritual but not religious, or simply open to deeper reflection, this book offers a path of practical spiritual engagement rooted in global wisdom traditions and timeless practices. Each weekly practice invites you to pause, reflect, and act, cultivating wholeness, clarity, and transformation from the inside out.

We live in an age of chronic busyness, relentless distraction, and spiritual drought. Many of us feel untethered, cut off from a more profound sense of purpose, peace, or connection. Over the past eighteen months, I endured one of the most spiritually devastating seasons of my life. It was disorienting, painful, and humbling. The inner framework I had relied upon crumbled, leaving me raw and uncertain. In that vulnerable space, I became fiercely determined to awaken and thrive. I knew that spiritual strength was what I needed to overcome my challenges.

So, I searched. I turned to sacred texts, ancient philosophies, and cutting-edge research. I spoke with wise elders, scholars, and everyday mystics. I studied, prayed, wept, doubted, and practiced. I gathered spiritual tools from around the world, encompassing Indigenous ceremonies, contemplative silence, Sufi poetry, and Buddhist breathwork. I tested each one in the crucible of personal suffering, not as an academic exercise but as a desperate quest for meaning. And what I discovered is that spiritual resilience is not reserved for saints or sages; spiritual resilience is built through small, consistent, and intentional practices.

Human flourishing is a holistic concept, encompassing the mental, emotional, physical, social, and spiritual dimensions. Across disciplines and cultures, research confirms that our well-being depends on nurturing all these domains. And yet, our spiritual health, however we define it, is often the most neglected. We may dismiss it as irrelevant, too religious, too vague, or too time-consuming. But the whole self suffers when our spirit is starved.

For some, spirituality has been confused with dogma or confined to rigid belief systems. For others, it feels abstract, inaccessible, or disconnected from everyday life. These devotional bridges that gap. Here, spirituality is not a doctrinal memorization but a practice to be lived. It is something we do over time, with intention, just as a physician practices medicine or an artist practices her craft. If we want to cultivate spiritual vitality, we must be willing to show up and engage.

These pages contain practices I researched, refined, and lived through in my darkest hours. They are not trends or theoretical models. They are grounded tools drawn from diverse traditions that helped me recalibrate and rediscover joy amidst life's chaos. I hope that they will do the same for you.

No matter your background or beliefs, this journey is for you. Whether you call it Spirit, Source, God, the Universe, or simply a deeper Self, what matters is your willingness to explore. If you devote yourself to one practice each week for the next 52 weeks, I believe you will uncover strength you didn't know you had, insights that surprise you, and a sense of inner connection that transcends any single tradition.

I offer no promises of perfection within these pages. However, if you apply these practices, spiritual growth will occur. Some practices may challenge you; others may resonate immediately. I simply ask that you approach this process with an open mind. Try each practice for seven days. Let curiosity replace judgment. Be gentle with yourself. See what stirs.

How to Use This Book

Awaken is organized as a yearlong guide, with one practice for each week. Each chapter starts by introducing the week's theme and its cultural, spiritual, or philosophical background. You'll then find a short reflection to help you focus and set your intention. Every practice comes with simple, clear steps you can use right away. The practices are not meant to be overwhelming, but rather to gently disrupt the automatic mode of daily life, creating space for inner realignment. At the end of each chapter, you'll find a reflective prompt and journaling space. Use it freely as a container for thoughts, drawings, questions, or prayers. There are no correct answers here, only your experience.

You can follow the book sequentially or skip ahead to the practices that resonate with your current season. Trust your discernment. Let this book be a companion, not a checklist. Modify what you need. Skip what doesn't serve you. Return to what moves you.

Most importantly, you are not alone. I will be walking this path right alongside you. I invite you to engage with me and others to share insights, celebrate growth, and support one another on the same journey. Together, we are cultivating lives of deeper resilience, presence, and sacred purpose.

So, take a breath. Settle into this invitation. Try one practice. Just one. Let that first step be enough.

Take a deep breath. Be willing to take a risk and try something new, even if it feels awkward at first. Commit to one week, one practice, and see what stirs awake in you. There is so much more to life than mere survival and living life on autopilot, and I look forward to you discovering it.

1
THE GROUNDING BREATH (INSPIRED BY ZEN BUDDHISM)

Breathing in long, one knows: I breathe in long; breathing out long, one knows: I breathe out long...I will breathe out, sensitive to the entire body...I breathe in calming...I breathe out calming.

—ANAPANASATI SUTTA, MAJJHIMA NIKAYA 118

In the fast-paced world we live in, the mind gets pulled in countless directions by cell phones, emails, work, relationships, memories, fears, and obligations. Amidst the mental noise, one simple yet profound tool is always available: the breath. Breath is a constant companion. Returning attention to your breath helps quiet mental clutter and invites a sense of calmness and clarity. It roots you in the present moment.

Grounded breathing has been central in traditions like Zen Buddhism for centuries. Rather than manipulating or forcing the breath, you observe it as it is. As Zen master Thich Nhat Hanh reminds us, "Conscious breathing is my anchor."* This kind of pres-

---

* Thich Nhat Hanh, *Peace Is Every Step: The Path of Mindfulness in Everyday Life* (New York: Bantam Books, 1992), 19.

ence isn't limited to any single tradition; it's part of being human. Science now confirms what many ancient paths have long taught: paying attention to the breath can calm the body, ease stress, and help us feel more emotionally grounded. In a world that constantly tugs at our attention, this practice draws us back to center to a quieter, steadier place of steadiness, presence, and peace.

Grounded breathing is a powerful tool for inner stillness and alignment. When you slow down and observe each inhale and exhale, you start to interrupt the automatic responses that often shape your thoughts, emotions, and reactions. By noticing the inhale and exhale, we begin to train our minds toward gentleness and presence. This practice cultivates what some traditions refer to as *witness consciousness*. Witness consciousness is the ability to observe without clinging, resisting, or judging. Over time, grounded breathing becomes more than a calming tool; it becomes a ritual of reconnection, reconnecting you with yourself again and again.

Grounded breathing is rooted deeply in the Zen Buddhist tradition. The origins can be found in early Buddhist texts, such as the *Anapanasati Sutta* from the *Pali Canon*. Over centuries, Zen developed this teaching into *zazen*. *Zazen*, or seated meditation, is a practice where practitioners sit in stillness, observing their breath and allowing their thoughts to pass without attachment. While the tradition is spiritual, the practice itself is universal. Everyone breathes, regardless of religion, culture, or worldview, making this a powerful, non-sectarian tool for cultivating grounding, presence, and inner balance.

Weekly Practice: Grounded Breathing

Each day this week, set aside at least five minutes to practice mindful breathing. You can do this at any time, such as first thing in the morning, during a lunch break, or whenever you feel anxious or distracted.

INSTRUCTIONS:

1. Sit comfortably, upright but relaxed.
2. Rest your hands on your thighs or fold them gently in your lap.
3. Close your eyes if that feels natural to you.
4. Notice your breath entering and leaving through your nose.
5. As you breathe, silently say to yourself:
    - *"Breathing in, I know I am breathing in."*
    - *"Breathing out, I know I am breathing out."*
6. If your mind wanders (and it will), notice that, and return your focus to the breath—no judgment, just awareness.

Try this practice daily. It may seem small, but over time, it builds emotional steadiness and deeper presence.

Breathing is with you wherever you go. By practicing awareness of the breath, you begin to cultivate spiritual resilience in a simple, universal way. Whenever you feel overwhelmed, remember you can return to your breath. That is where you will find your ground.

Reflection Journal

Day 1

- What did I notice during my breathing practice today?
- One insight or feeling.
- My intention for tomorrow.

_____
_____
_____
_____
_____

Day 2

- What distracted me most during today's breathing practice? *(Was it thoughts, sounds, emotions, restlessness?)*
- One insight or feeling.
- My intention for tomorrow.

_____
_____
_____
_____
_____
_____
_____
_____
_____

Day 3

- How did my body feel before and after the practice? *(Notice any changes in tension, posture, or breath)*
- One insight or feeling.
- My intention for tomorrow.

_____
_____
_____
_____
_____
_____
_____
_____
_____

Day 4

- What emotions surfaced during my breath awareness today? *(Was there calm, resistance, sadness, gratitude, etc.?)*
- One insight or feeling:
- My intention for tomorrow.

_____
_____
_____
_____
_____
_____
_____
_____

Day 5

- What helped me stay present with my breath today? *(Did you use a phrase, visualization, or body awareness?)*
- One insight or feeling.
- My intention for tomorrow.

_____
_____
_____
_____
_____
_____
_____
_____

Day 6

- How has this breathing practice affected me this week? *(Reflect on any inner shifts or outer changes you noticed)*
- One insight or feeling.
- My intention moving forward.

_____
_____
_____
_____
_____
_____
_____
_____
_____

Day 7: End-of-Week Reflection

- Look back over your journal entries from this week, then take time today to reflect deeply on your overall experience.
- What have I learned about myself through the practice of grounded breathing? *(You might reflect on how your body responded, how your mind wandered, how you showed yourself grace, or any unexpected insights that surfaced.)*
- What moments stood out or felt meaningful during the week? *(Was there a breath that calmed you? A moment of stillness? A shift in emotion?)*
- How might I carry this practice forward in my daily life? *(Set a gentle intention for how and when you'll continue using breath as an anchor in stressful or ordinary moments.)*

Awaken

2
THE CENTERING PRAYER (INSPIRED BY CHRISTIAN MYSTICISM)

Silence is God's first language; everything else is a poor translation.

— THOMAS KEATING

Centering Prayer is a silent contemplative prayer that leads us beyond words, thoughts, and emotions into a deeper communion with the Divine. Practiced by choosing a sacred word such as "peace," "love," or "God." We return to this word whenever we are distracted, not as a mantra to control the mind, but as a symbol of intention and consent to the divine presence. The practice typically lasts 10-20 minutes and is repeated daily. It is not meant to replace other forms of prayer but to deepen one's receptivity to grace through interior silence.*

Centering Prayer is an ancient Christian practice that leads us into a state of stillness. It has its roots in the early desert mystics, those wise, wandering souls who sought God in silence and were later shaped by the contemplative rhythms of Cistercian monks. At its

---

* Thomas Keating, *Open Mind, Open Heart: The Contemplative Dimension of the Gospel* (New York: Continuum, 2006), 19.

heart, this practice is simple: we choose a sacred word and let it draw us inward, helping us rest in the quiet presence of the Divine, beyond thoughts, beyond striving. Unlike discursive prayer or vocal petitions, this method is a contemplative gesture of surrender rather than effort.

Rooted in the 14th-century mystical text *The Cloud of Unknowing*, Centering Prayer calls the seeker to "lift up their heart to God with a meek stirring of love" and surrender all concepts and images of the Divine into a "cloud of forgetting."* This is a path of mystical unknowing, where God is approached beyond the bounds of words. While rooted in Christian mysticism, it serves as a universal invitation into interior silence, love, and trust. It is a form of prayer that does not seek to grasp the Divine but to be grasped by the Divine.† This approach to prayer resonates with practices in other religious traditions such as Buddhist *mindfulness*, Hindu *japa* (repetitive prayer), and Sufi *dhikr* (remembrance), all of which emphasize interior stillness and the transcendence of ego. In this way, Centering Prayer becomes a universal doorway to contemplation, accessible to spiritual seekers across diverse paths.

Weekly Practice: Centering Prayer

This week, commit to a simple daily rhythm of Centering Prayer. Set aside 10–20 minutes each day to cultivate inner stillness and presence.

INSTRUCTIONS:

1. Choose a sacred word that resonates with your heart (e.g., *peace, love, hope*).

---

* Anonymous, *The Cloud of Unknowing*, trans. Carmen Acevedo Butcher (Boston: Shambhala, 2009), 39–41.
† Cynthia Bourgeault, *Centering Prayer and Inner Awakening* (Cambridge, MA: Cowley Publications, 2004), 16-17.

2. Sit comfortably, close your eyes, and gently rest your attention on that word.
3. When thoughts arise (as they naturally will), return to the word, without judgment.
4. Conclude your session with a moment of gratitude or a deep breath of awareness.

In the stillness of Centering Prayer, you may begin to encounter "the peace of God, which surpasses all understanding" (Phil. 4:7, ESV). This sacred silence invites you to release the grip of ego, fear, and striving.

Reflection Journal

Day 1

- What sacred word did I choose, and why does it resonate with me today?
- What distractions arose during the prayer time?
- How did I feel when I gently returned to the word?

_____
_____
_____
_____
_____
_____
_____
_____
_____
_____

Day 2

- Did I feel any resistance to entering silence today?
- What sensations did I notice in my body during the practice?
- Did I experience any sense of connection, peace, or discomfort?

_____
_____
_____
_____
_____
_____
_____
_____

Day 3

- Was my focus deeper or more scattered today compared to earlier in the week?
- Did any unexpected thoughts, memories, or emotions arise?
- How did I respond internally to those moments?

_____
_____
_____
_____
_____
_____

Day 4

- What was different about today's prayer experience?
- Did I feel a sense of presence, stillness, or absence?
- How did this time of quiet affect the rest of my day?

Day 5

- How has my relationship with the sacred word evolved?
- Did I feel more aware of my inner world today?
- What emotional or spiritual shifts (if any) did I notice?

Day 6

- What inner posture or attitude did I bring to prayer today?
- Was it harder or easier to enter into silence? Why?
- What word or image best describes today's experience?

Day 7

- What was the most surprising or meaningful moment I experienced during Centering Prayer this week?
- How did the practice impact my mind, emotions, or spiritual awareness over time?
- In what ways has my perception of silence changed?
- What did I learn about myself through this practice?

3

WALKING MEDITATION (INSPIRED BY THERAVADA BUDDHISM)

Walk as if you are kissing the earth with your feet.

— THICH NHAT HANH

Walking meditation is about paying attention to each step you take. Instead of moving on autopilot, you slow down and feel your feet touching the ground, notice your breath, and become aware of your body in motion. It's a simple way to come back to the present moment. For many people, especially those who struggle with sitting still, this moving meditation can feel more natural. It brings the mind and body into sync, creating space for calmness, clarity, and a deeper sense of connection.

Your feet can become instruments of peace. Each step is a chance to return to yourself, to this very moment. Walking meditation, known as *cankama* in the Theravāda Buddhist tradition, is an ancient practice that transforms everyday movement into a means of awakening. It's a reminder that presence isn't only found in stillness; it can move with us. Every step becomes an opportunity to return home to ourselves. Whether you're walking through a forest, a garden, or just down a quiet hallway, this simple practice helps the mind slow down and the heart open up.

Walking meditation dates to early Buddhism. In the *Satipatthāna Sutta* (MN 10) of the *Pāli Canon*, the Buddha encouraged his monks to stay mindful whether they were walking, sitting, standing, or lying down. In the Theravāda tradition, it's often used between seated meditation sessions to help carry that awareness into movement. It's a beautiful reminder that mindfulness isn't just something we find in stillness; it can move with us, step by step, through ordinary life.

Weekly Practice: Walking Meditation

This week, devote at least 10 minutes each day to mindful walking. Let each step be a meditation that returns you to the present moment.

INSTRUCTIONS:

1. Begin by standing still. Take a few breaths and gently bring your attention to your body.
2. Start walking slowly. Feel each foot as it lifts, moves through space, and touches the ground.
3. With each step, silently say to yourself: *"lifting... moving... placing."* This keeps the mind in sync with the rhythm of your body.
4. alk in a small space (a hallway, garden path, or room), allowing you to focus inward without rushing or wandering too far.
5. If your mind drifts, simply return to your breath and your steps.

Walking meditation reminds us that inner peace is not limited. We don't have to be sitting in a quiet room or in complete silence. Meditation can occur in motion; with every breath and every step we take. It teaches us to slow down and notice that the sacred is already here and present with us and within us.

Reflection Journal

Day 1

- What did I notice as I slowed down my steps?
- Did walking mindfully feel natural or awkward today?
- How did I feel afterward—physically, mentally, or emotionally?

_____
_____
_____
_____
_____
_____
_____
_____

Day 2

- What sensations did I notice in my feet, legs, or breath?
- Was it hard to stay focused? What distracted me?
- How did I respond when my mind wandered?

_____
_____
_____

Day 3

- Did walking this way affect my mood or energy?
- What was different about today's practice compared to yesterday?
- Did I feel more connected to my body or surroundings?

Day 4

- Was it easier or harder to stay present today?
- Did any emotions arise during the walk?
- What did I learn from simply observing my steps?

Day 5

- What helped me stay grounded during the walk today?
- Did I feel rushed, relaxed, or something else entirely?
- How did this practice affect the rest of my day?

Day 6

- What felt most meaningful about today's walk?
- Did I experience moments of peace or spaciousness?
- If my attention drifted, how did I return to the practice?

Day 7: End-of-Week Reflection

- How has this practice shaped my awareness of the present moment?
- What have I learned about my mind, body, or inner world while walking?
- In what ways has this form of meditation affected my mood, stress, or spiritual life?
- How does mindful walking compare to other forms of stillness or prayer I've practiced?
- Will I continue this practice beyond this week?

Awaken

4

THE GRATITUDE JAR (INSPIRED BY RELIGION AND SOCIAL PSYCHOLOGY)

Gratitude is, first and foremost, a way of seeing that alters our gaze.

— ROBERT EMMONS

It is easy to get stuck in a loop of negative thoughts. For example, what's not working, what's hurting, what we wish would change, etc. Sometimes, we don't even realize we are doing it. However, gratitude is a practice that interrupts that negative thought cycle. Gratitude shifts our attention toward what's already good, what's holding us up, and what gives us hope and purpose even in the midst of hardship and the struggles of life. Gratitude doesn't deny pain; it just doesn't allow troubled times to define the situation.

The act of giving thanks is a timeless tradition. Gratitude is woven into nearly every spiritual and religious tradition worldwide. From psalms of praise in the Hebrew Bible to daily meal blessings in Jewish and Christian practice, gratitude has always been a way to realign the heart with something greater than ourselves. In many Indigenous cultures, giving thanks to the land, ancestors, and elements is not a ritual; it's a lifelong practice of gratitude.

Modern psychology now confirms what spiritual traditions have taught since the beginning of time. Both spiritual and psychological evidence suggest that gratitude helps reduce anxiety and depression, fosters emotional resilience, and enhances our ability to cope with life's challenges.* The Gratitude Jar is a visual way to practice gratitude and helps build a habit of noticing what is good. Each note becomes a kind of offering, a written reminder that there is beauty in the everyday.

Weekly Practice: The Gratitude Jar

This week, create a Gratitude Jar. A small daily ritual that helps anchor your awareness on what is good and true.
Instructions:

1. Select a jar, box, or container that holds meaning or beauty for you. Place it somewhere visible.
2. Each day, write down one thing you're grateful for on a small slip of paper.
3. Place the note in the jar. You can say it aloud as a prayer or affirmation if that feels right.
4. At the end of the week, open the jar and read each note.

Gratitude reminds us that even in the struggle, there's something good, something to be grateful for, and something worth returning to. Whether it's a moment of laughter, the kindness of a stranger, or the breath in your lungs, these are not small things. The more we name them, the more they multiply. Gratitude doesn't just change how we feel; it changes how we see.

---

* Greater Good Science Center, "Gratitude," University of California, Berkeley, https://greatergood.berkeley.edu/topic/gratitude/definition.
 Robert A. Emmons and Michael E. McCullough, "Counting Blessings Versus Burdens: An Experimental Investigation of Gratitude and Subjective Well-Being in Daily Life," *Journal of Personality and Social Psychology* 84, no. 2 (2003): 377–89.

Reflection Journal

Day 1

- What did I choose to write down today?
- How did it feel to pause and name something good?
- Did anything shift in my mood or mindset afterward?

_____
_____
_____
_____
_____
_____
_____

Day 2

- Was it easy or hard to think of something to be grateful for today? Why?
- How did writing it down feel in my body?
- Did the act of gratitude bring up any unexpected emotions?

_____
_____
_____
_____
_____
_____
_____

Day 3

- What was different about today's note compared to yesterday?
- Did I feel more present or connected afterward?
- How does my Gratitude Jar look or feel at this point in the week?

_____
_____
_____
_____
_____
_____
_____
_____
_____

Day 4

- What did I notice about the small things today?
- Did I take anything for granted before I paused to give thanks?
- What impact is this practice starting to have?

_____
_____
_____
_____
_____
_____
_____
_____

Day 5

- What was I grateful for today that surprised me?
- Did writing it down deepen the feeling of gratitude?
- How might this practice be shaping my perspective?

_____
_____
_____
_____
_____
_____
_____
_____

Day 6

- Was there a moment today when I felt truly grateful, even briefly?
- How has this week altered my perspective on my everyday life?
- What's one thing I've realized through this practice?

_____
_____
_____
_____
_____
_____
_____
_____

Day 7

- What patterns did I notice in the things I wrote down?
- How did the daily act of naming gratitude affect my mood, energy, or sense of connection?
- Did anything about this practice challenge me? Surprise me?
- In what ways do I want to carry this gratitude practice forward?
- What am I most thankful for in this moment?

5

BODY SCAN AWARENESS (INSPIRED BY VIPASSANA MEDITATION)

In this body, there is the path to awakening.

— *MAHĀSATIPAṬṬHĀNA SUTTA, DĪGHA NIKĀYA* 22

Many of us spend most of our time in our heads, thinking, analyzing, and worrying, forgetting that our bodies are where we actually reside. Stress, distractions, and constant motion can disconnect us from our own physical home. The body scan is a traditional practice from *vipassanā* (insight) meditation that guides our attention back into the body. It invites us to notice sensations, tensions, and patterns without judgment or the need to change anything. Once we learn to scan our body with patience and curiosity, we begin to release stress, cultivate self-acceptance, and build resilience from the inside out.

Body scan meditation has its roots in the Buddhist insight tradition, particularly in the *Mahāsatipaṭṭhāna Sutta* (DN 22), which outlines the Four Foundations of Mindfulness. The first of these foundations is mindfulness of the body, an invitation to pay close attention to physical sensations as a way of understanding impermanence and loosening the grip of attachment.

Today, body scan meditation is also central to many secular mindfulness programs, particularly Mindfulness-Based Stress Reduction (MBSR), which was founded by Jon Kabat-Zinn.*These programs have adapted ancient practices to support healing and stress relief in modern life. But the wisdom remains the same: coming home to the body will lead to presence, compassion, and awakening.

Weekly Practice: Body Scan Meditation

This week, you'll practice a daily body scan to reconnect with your body and cultivate mindful awareness.

INSTRUCTION:

1. Lie down or sit comfortably in a quiet space.
2. Close your eyes and take a few deep breaths.
3. Bring your attention to your feet. Notice any sensations, warmth, tingling, or tension.
4. Slowly move your awareness upward through your legs, hips, back, shoulders, arms, neck, and head.
5. If you notice tension, gently breathe into that area. No need to fix—just notice.
6. If your mind wanders (and it will), return your attention to the next area of the body.

Your body is not your enemy. It's your home and your anchor to the present moment. When you learn to scan the body with curiosity instead of criticism, you begin to reclaim something sacred. A sense of wholeness, safety, and peace that's been there all along, just waiting for you to notice.

---

* Jon Kabat-Zinn, *Full Catastrophe Living: Using the Wisdom of Your Body and Mind to Face Stress, Pain, and Illness*(New York: Bantam Dell, 1990).

Reflection Journal

Day 1

- What did I notice in my body today?
- Was it challenging to stay present?
- How do I feel after completing the scan?

_____
_____
_____
_____
_____
_____
_____
_____
_____

Day 2

- Were there any areas that held more tension or emotion?
- Did I judge what I felt, or did I allow it to be?
- What helped me stay focused?

_____
_____
_____
_____
_____
_____
_____
_____
_____

Day 3

- How did my awareness shift throughout the practice?
- Was there a moment of stillness or connection?
- What surprised me today?

_____
_____
_____
_____
_____
_____
_____
_____

Day 4

- Did I feel more embodied or grounded after the practice?
- How does my body feel compared to how it felt earlier this week?
- What emotions surfaced, if any?

_____
_____
_____
_____
_____
_____
_____
_____

Day 5

- Which part of the body felt most present today?
- Did anything shift in how I relate to discomfort or tension?
- How can I apply this awareness to my daily life?

_____
_____
_____
_____
_____
_____
_____
_____

Day 6

- What was different about today's scan?
- How does my body want to be treated after this practice?
- What's one thing I'm learning from listening to my body?

_____
_____
_____
_____
_____
_____
_____
_____

Day 7

- How has my relationship with my body shifted during this week?
- What patterns or insights emerged through the daily practice?
- Did I experience any change in how I respond to tension or discomfort?
- In what ways has this practice supported my sense of wholeness or peace?
- Will I continue body scanning beyond this week? Why or why not?

6
LOVING-KINDNESS MEDITATION (INSPIRED BY METTA, BUDDHIST)

May all beings be happy. May all beings be safe. May all beings be peaceful.

— METTA SUTTA, SAṀYUTTA NIKĀYA 1.8

One of the most effective tools for cultivating a resilient heart is the practice of loving-kindness meditation. This meditation practice is known as *metta* in the Buddhist tradition. *Metta* is an ancient practice that expands goodwill outward —from yourself to loved ones, to strangers, and even to those who are difficult to love. It softens our hearts and helps us see our shared humanity more clearly. Loving-kindness is a training of the heart. It teaches us to choose compassion over fear, to break down barriers, and to remember that love is not just a feeling; it's a practice.

Metta meditation is described in the Metta Sutta (SN 1.8) of the Pāli Canon, where the Buddha encourages the development of boundless love that extends in all directions without exception. Practiced regularly, *metta* has been shown to increase empathy, reduce anger, and even improve physical and emotional well-being.*

While rooted in Theravāda Buddhism, the spirit of this practice resonates across faiths. It echoes the Christian tradition of intercessory prayer, the Jewish greeting *shalom aleichem* (peace be upon you), and the Islamic invocation of *rahma* (mercy). Across cultures, there is a deep recognition that wishing well for others shapes who we become.

Weekly Practice: Loving-Kindness Meditation

This week, you'll practice daily *metta* meditation, cultivating loving-kindness for yourself and others.

INSTRUCTIONS:

1. Sit comfortably and close your eyes. Begin by taking a few deep breaths.
2. Silently repeat the following phrases:
    - *May I be happy. May I be healthy. May I be safe. May I live with ease.*
3. Bring to mind someone you love. Offer them the exact phrases.
4. Next, picture someone neutral (like a neighbor or cashier). Repeat the phrases for them.
5. Now, think of someone you find difficult, and offer them the same loving kindness.
6. End by expanding your intention to all beings everywhere:
    - *May all beings be happy. May all beings live with ease.*

---

* Barbara L. Fredrickson, Bethany C. Kok, et al., "Open Hearts Build Lives: Positive Emotions, Induced Through Loving-Kindness Meditation, Build Consequential Personal Resources," *Journal of Personality and Social Psychology* 95, no. 5 (2008): 1045–1062.

Metta is like planting and watering seeds of love inside your own heart. You may not see growth right away, but something shifts. Over time, those seeds bloom into patience, compassion, and the kind of peace that doesn't depend on perfect circumstances. Even in a broken world, you can still choose love. And that choice changes everything.

Reflection Journal

Day 1

- How did I feel offering kindness to myself?
- Was it easy or hard to stay present with the phrases?
- What did I notice in my body or emotions?

_____

_____

_____

_____

_____

_____

_____

_____

_____

_____

Day 2

- Who did I choose as my "loved one" today? Why?
- What emotions came up while offering them kindness?
- Did anything shift in how I felt afterward?

_____

_____

_____

Day 3

- How did it feel to direct kindness to a neutral person?
- Did I experience any resistance or openness?
- What did this teach me about my perceptions of others?

Day 4

- Who was the "difficult person" I included today?
- Was it challenging to offer them loving kindness?
- Did I notice judgment, compassion, or something else?

Day 5

- How did I feel while offering *metta* to all beings?
- Did the practice feel expansive, emotional, or flat?
- What message did I need to hear most today?

Day 6

- What patterns have I observed in my interactions with different people during this practice?
- Has anything shifted in my heart, emotions, or relationships?
- What surprised me most about this week?

_____
_____
_____
_____
_____
_____
_____
_____
_____

Day 7

- How has this practice shaped the way I relate to myself?
- What was the most challenging part of the practice? What was most healing?
- How did it feel to include someone I find challenging?
- Did the practice make any difference in my daily interactions?
- Will I continue practicing *metta*? What would help me stay consistent?

_____
_____
_____
_____

7

SACRED LISTENING (INSPIRED BY QUAKER TRADITION)

Listen deeply, so that others may hear their own truth. *

— *UNKNOWN*

Let's face it, most of us enjoy hearing ourselves talk. Our world is a place that values speaking, having answers, making points, and filling silence. But what would it mean to truly listen? To listen without interrupting, without fixing, without needing to be right? Sacred listening, rooted in Quaker practice, is about creating a quiet, welcoming space where someone can speak from the heart and feel fully seen. The Quakers describe this as *"holding someone in the Light,"* which means you are offering your full attention with care and reverence.† When we slow down and listen in this way, something holy happens. The noise fades, and the connection becomes possible.

In the Quaker tradition (also known as the Religious Society of

---

* Quoted in Parker J. Palmer, *A Hidden Wholeness: The Journey Toward an Undivided Life* (San Francisco: Jossey-Bass, 2004), 120.
† "What Do Quakers Mean by 'Holding Someone in the Light'?" QuakerInfo.org, accessed July 17, 2025, https://www.quakerinfo.org/light.shtml.

Friends), silence is not an absence; it's a presence. In *Meetings for Worship*, Quakers gather not to recite prayers or follow a sermon, but to wait in shared stillness. When someone feels led by the Spirit, they speak. The rest listen; not to argue or analyze, but to receive.* This practice of communal, Spirit-led listening has evolved into what some refer to as "clearness committees" or spiritual accompaniment. Clearness committees are a non-directive way of helping others discern their inner truth. Sacred listening is deeply aligned with the Quaker value of equality: every voice matters, and every person holds inner wisdom. Similar forms of intentional listening also appear in Indigenous talking circles, pastoral care, and chaplaincy work.

Weekly Practice: Sacred Listening

This week, practice sacred listening each day in conversations, in moments of silence, and even with yourself.

INSTRUCTIONS:

1. In your conversations, pause before responding. Focus entirely on listening.
2. Let go of interrupting, correcting, or rehearsing what you'll say next.
3. If it feels natural, reflect on what you heard—not to fix, but to affirm.
4. Internally, hold the person "in the Light," a Quaker phrase for listening with love and respect.
5. After the conversation, take a moment to reflect on what you learned, not just about them, but about yourself.

Sacred listening is one of the most generous things you can offer

---

* Douglas Gwyn, *The Covenant Crucified: Quakers and the Rise of Capitalism* (Wallingford, PA: Pendle Hill Publications, 1995), 18–22.

to another person. When you listen with an open heart, without trying to fix or change someone, you create space for them to hear themselves more clearly. Sacred listening isn't just about hearing words; it's about witnessing a soul. And in that quietness, something sacred unfolds.

Reflection Journal

Day 1

- Who did I listen to today?
- What was it like to focus only on receiving their words?
- Did anything shift in how I usually respond?

_____
_____
_____
_____
_____
_____
_____
_____

Day 2

- What was challenging about staying quiet or not offering advice?
- How did the other person respond to being fully heard?
- How did I feel during and after the interaction?

_____
_____

Day 3

- Did I notice any moments where I wanted to interrupt?
- What helped me stay grounded in listening?
- What did this conversation reveal about the other person —or me?

Day 4

- Who did I hold in the Light today, and why?
- What did I notice when I listened with compassion instead of judgment?

- How might I bring this presence into more of my relationships?

Day 5.

- Was there a moment of silence in conversation today that felt meaningful?
- What would it look like to listen to myself this way?
- What surprised me about today's listening experience?

DAY 6

- How has my listening changed this week?
- Have others responded differently to me?
- What am I learning about presence, patience, or connection?

DAY 7

- What impact did this practice have on my relationships?
- Did I notice any internal shifts—more patience, empathy, or stillness?
- What was the most meaningful or challenging part of listening this way?
- How did it feel to hold someone "in the Light"?
- Will I continue this practice in some form?

8
NATURE AS SANCTUARY (INSPIRED BY CELTIC SPIRITUALITY)

The earth is full of thresholds where the divine leaks through.

— JOHN O'DONOHUE

Modern life often keeps us disconnected from the natural world and trapped indoors, glued to screens, surrounded by noise and artificial light. But throughout history, nature has been a sacred place of renewal, a living cathedral under the sky. In Celtic spirituality, the land, sea, and sky are not just scenery; they are alive with sacred presence. When we step outside and pay attention, we cross those thresholds and remember we are part of something holy.

The ancient Celts believed that the natural world was filled with spirit and wisdom. The groves, rivers, stones, and animals were viewed not as objects, but as sacred, each with its connection to the Divine.* Nature wasn't just a backdrop for spiritual practice; it was the sacred space itself. This way of relating to the land resonates with

---

* "Relationship with Nature," The Order of Bards, Ovates & Druids, accessed July 17, 2025, https://druidry.org/druid-way/what-druidry/relationship-nature.

Indigenous traditions worldwide, where the earth is revered as a teacher, healer, and sometimes a relative. In modern Celtic-inspired paths, such as Druidry and eco-spirituality, this reverence is carried forward in rituals, poetry, and everyday life. Spending time in nature becomes more than a break; it becomes a spiritual return.

Weekly Practice: Nature as Sanctuary

This week, let nature become your sanctuary. Spend 20–30 minutes outside each day, not to exercise or produce something, but to be present and receive.
Instructions:

1. Leave your phone behind or turn it off completely.
2. Walk slowly or find a quiet place to sit in nature—this could be a forest, a beach, a garden, or even a tree-lined sidewalk.
3. Observe with all your senses: What do you see, hear, smell, and feel?
4. Silently thank the earth for sustaining you. Offer your presence in return.
5. If you feel drawn, collect a small natural object (a stone, leaf, shell) to carry with you as a sacred reminder.

Nature is not just something we walk through; it is something that sustains us and something we belong to. When we spend time outdoors with open eyes and an open heart, we remember what the ancients knew: the earth is alive, and it speaks to us. Returning to the living world helps us return to ourselves. The forest, the wind, the water, they're not separate from spirit. They are spirit, calling us to awaken.

Reflection Journal

Day 1

- Where did I go today, and what did I notice first?
- How did being in nature affect my mind or body?
- Did anything feel sacred, even in a small way?

Day 2

- What sounds or textures stood out to me today?
- Did I feel more connected to myself or something greater?
- How did I relate to the space around me?

Day 3

- What was different about today's time outdoors?
- Did I notice any moments of beauty or peace?
- What did nature teach me today?

Day 4

- Was there a particular place or object that drew my attention?
- How did my energy shift during or after the time outside?
- What would it mean to treat the earth as sacred?

Day 5

- Did I feel a sense of belonging in the natural world today?
- What emotions surfaced while I was outside?
- What role does nature play in my spiritual life right now?

Day 6

- How have I changed since the beginning of the week?
- What parts of nature felt familiar or new today?
- What did I notice about my pace, breath, or thoughts?

Day 7

- What has this week in nature taught me about presence?
- How did the natural world reflect something about my inner world?
- Did I feel more spiritually connected, grounded, or alive?
- What will I carry forward from this practice into my daily life?
- How can I continue to honor nature as a sacred sanctuary?

9

THE MORNING OFFERING (INSPIRED BY HINDUISM)

Therefore, without attachment, perform always the work that has to be done, for a person who does their duty without attachment attains the Supreme.

— BHAGAVAD GITA 3.19

Each morning brings renewal and an opportunity to start anew. In the Hindu tradition, the day typically begins with a small act of devotion such as lighting a lamp, offering flowers, and reciting a prayer. These gestures may seem small, but they carry a profound meaning that aligns the heart with service, compassion, and gratitude before the world's rush begins. This is the spirit of *karma yoga,* selfless action offered as a sacred act. Whether or not you follow the Hindu path, this practice invites you to dedicate your day with clarity and intention.

In Hinduism, mornings are considered especially sacred. It's a time when the mind is quiet, the day is still open, and the spirit is receptive. Many traditional Hindu households begin the day with a *puja*, a ritual of offering flowers, water, or prayer at a home altar.* This isn't about complexity or dogma; it's about presence, reverence, and devotion.

The *Bhagavad Gita*, a central text in Hindu philosophy, teaches that we can turn even the most ordinary actions into sacred offerings when they are done without attachment.† This approach, known as *karma yoga*, is about offering our work, relationships, and efforts to the greater good. This concept can be easily adapted into any spiritual or secular practice. Morning offerings become a way to ground the day in love, intention, and humility.

Weekly Practice: The Morning Offering

This week, begin each morning with a personal offering. You don't need a temple, just a few quiet moments and an open heart.

INSTRUCTIONS:

1. Upon waking, take a few quiet breaths before reaching for your phone or starting your routine.
2. Think of one word that expresses your intention for the day (e.g., *kindness, peace, service*).
3. Silently say: *"I offer my day to [your word]."*
4. If it helps you focus, consider lighting a candle, burning incense, or placing your hand over your heart.
5. Carry that intention with you throughout the day—not as pressure, but as quiet guidance.

Every morning presents an opportunity to choose how you will approach the day. By beginning with a simple offering, you remind

---

* Eknath Easwaran, *The Bhagavad Gita for Daily Living, Vol. 1: The End of Sorrow* (Tomales, CA: Nilgiri Press, 2007), 41–44.
† Ibid.

yourself that even the smallest actions can be sacred. Whether it's lighting a candle or whispering a word of kindness. What you offer at dawn has the power to shape everything that follows.

Reflective Journal

Day 1

- What word did I choose today, and why?
- How did it feel to start the day with that intention?
- Did it influence how I moved through the day?

_____
_____
_____
_____
_____
_____
_____
_____

Day 2

- Did I remember my morning offering throughout the day?
- What moments aligned with my chosen word or intention?
- What challenges came up?

_____
_____
_____
_____

Day 3

- Was there anything sacred or symbolic about today's offering?
- How did my mood or energy shift after the practice?
- What did I learn about myself?

Day 4

- What intention rose naturally for me today?
- Did the act of offering feel meaningful or routine?
- What helped me stay centered today?

Day 5

- Did I encounter any moments where I acted from my offering?
- What helped me return to my intention when I felt distracted?
- How does this practice feel physically, emotionally, or spiritually?

Day 6

- What has been most meaningful about this practice so far?

- How have my mornings changed since beginning this?
- What does "offering" mean to me now?

Day 7

- What did I learn about intention and dedication this week?
- How did this practice impact the way I approached my daily tasks?
- Did anything shift in how I view service, work, or devotion?
- What spiritual or emotional benefits did I notice?
- Will I continue this morning ritual, or adapt it in a new way?

10

DAILY RESETS (INSPIRED BY STOICISM)

You have power over your mind — not outside events. Realize this, and you will find strength.

— MARCUS AURELIUS

With the amount of pressure, we often place upon ourselves, not to mention others, life can feel overwhelming. Thoughts spiral, emotions take over, and it's easy to feel like we have lost control before the day even begins. But the Stoic philosophers of ancient Greece and Rome offered a powerful tool: the daily reset. It's a practice of starting each day by returning to what matters most, what is in your control, what is not, and how you choose to respond. This kind of clarity does not just build mental discipline. It builds resilience, freedom, and peace.

Stoicism is a philosophy of practical wisdom, deeply rooted in the idea that virtue (living in alignment with reason and integrity) is the highest good. Figures like Epictetus, Seneca, and Marcus Aurelius all emphasized the importance of daily reflection. They suggest beginning and ending each day by checking in with your mind, your emotions, and your choices.*

Modern Stoic writers, like Ryan Holiday, have adapted these teachings for contemporary life, offering daily meditations that help ground us in courage, clarity, and self-responsibility.† Like many contemplative traditions, Stoicism reminds us that while we can't control what happens to us, we can always choose how we respond. That choice is where our authentic power lives.

Weekly Practice: Daily Rest

This week, start each morning with a daily Stoic-style reset. It doesn't take long—but it can change how you meet the day.

INSTRUCTIONS:

1. Sit quietly and take a few deep breaths to settle your mind.
2. Ask yourself two questions:
   - *What is in my control today?*
   - *What is not in my control?*
3. Visualize yourself gently releasing what is outside your control—like setting down a heavy bag.
4. Set one clear intention for the day, rooted in your values (e.g., patience, honesty, courage).
5. Carry that intention with you as a compass to navigate the day.

There is power in pausing before the day begins. Each morning, you have the opportunity to reset, letting go of what you can't control and recommitting to what you can. This is the heart of resilience. A

---

* Seneca, *Letters from a Stoic*, trans. Robin Campbell (New York: Penguin Classics, 2004), 70–72.
† Ryan Holiday and Stephen Hanselman, *The Daily Stoic: 366 Meditations on Wisdom, Perseverance, and the Art of Living* (New York: Portfolio, 2016).

foundation of resilience is understanding what is not in your control with clarity. When you start from this place, even the most ordinary day can become a meaningful day.

Reflection Journal

Day 1

- What did I identify as being in my control today?
- What did I let go of?
- What intention did I set?

Day 2

- Was it easy or hard to release what I can't control?
- How did my intention influence my day?
- What felt different about how I responded to challenges?

Day 3

- What unexpected thoughts or emotions came up during the reset?
- Did I remember my intention throughout the day?
- What would I like to carry forward into tomorrow?

Day 4

- What patterns do I notice in what's outside my control?
- How does naming what I can control affect my mindset?
- Did I stay aligned with my values today?

Day 5

- What situations tested my patience, and how did I respond?
- Did my intention help me stay centered or grounded?
- What do I need to remind myself of right now?

Day 6

- How has my relationship with control shifted this week?
- What values keep showing up in my reflections?
- What am I learning about myself through this practice?

Day 7

- What impact did this simple daily reset have on my mindset or emotions?
- How did it help me deal with stress, uncertainty, or frustration?
- What intention or value felt most important to me this week?
- Did I feel more in alignment with my deeper self?
- Will I continue this practice, or adapt it to fit my rhythm?

11

CHANTING (INSPIRED BY HINDU/BHAKTI TRADITION)

Constant remembrance of the name brings one into the presence of the Beloved.

— NARADA BHAKTI SUTRA, 82

Sound is vibration, and vibration is life. In the Bhakti traditions of Hinduism, chanting the names of the Divine is more than music; it's prayer, meditation, and surrender. Whether sung aloud or whispered in the heart, these sacred sounds carry the energy of devotion. Beyond religious context, repeating a sacred phrase or positive word can calm the mind, regulate the breath, and open the heart. Your voice becomes a bridge between your head and heart, between yourself and your spirit.

In *Bhakti Yoga*, the path of devotion, chanting is used as a way to express love for the Divine. This can take the form of *japa* (silent repetition), *kirtan* (call-and-response singing), or reciting a mantra.* Traditionally, devotees repeat sacred names such as *Rama, Krishna,* or

---

* Eknath Easwaran, *God Makes the Rivers to Flow* (Tomales, CA: Nilgiri Press, 2009), 26–30.

Om Namah Shivaya to quiet the mind and draw closer to God. But chanting as spiritual practice isn't unique to Hinduism. Gregorian chant in Christianity, *nigunim* in Judaism, and *dhikr* in Sufism are all ways people have used rhythm and repetition to steady the heart and remember what matters.* Whether you use a traditional mantra or a word like *peace* or *love*, sound can become sanctuary.

Weekly Practice: Chanting

This week, you'll explore chanting as a daily practice, either through sacred mantras or simple words of intention.

INSTRUCTIONS:

1. Choose a word or phrase to repeat. This might be a Sanskrit mantra (e.g., *Om Shanti, So Hum*) or an English word like *peace, hope,* or *I am loved*.
2. Sit comfortably and take a few deep breaths.
3. Begin to repeat the word aloud or silently for five minutes. You can chant rhythmically or speak in a slow, deliberate manner.
4. Feel the vibration in your chest, your breath, your body. Let your mind rest in the rhythm.
5. If your thoughts wander, return to the sound.

Chanting is not about having a perfect voice. Chanting is about using your voice to remember who you are. Whether through mantra, prayer, or a single loving word, repetition grounds the mind and opens the heart. Over time, the sound becomes more than simple sound. It becomes silence, presence, and peace.

---

* Llewellyn Vaughan-Lee, *The Music of the Soul: Sufi Teachings* (Inverness, CA: Golden Sufi Center, 1995), 12–15.

Reflection Journal

Day 1

- What mantra or word did I choose today?
- How did it feel to speak or hear the sound?
- What physical or emotional sensations did I notice?

_____
_____
_____
_____
_____
_____
_____
_____
_____

Day 2

- Was it easy or difficult to stay focused on the sound?
- Did the repetition affect my mood or energy?
- What meaning does this word or phrase hold for me?

_____
_____
_____
_____
_____
_____

Day 3

- What emotions arose during or after the practice?
- How did the sound feel in my body today?
- Did I feel more connected—spiritually, emotionally, or physically?

Day 4

- Did the repetition begin to feel natural or meditative?
- Was the practice more internal or expressive today?
- How did this session shape the rest of my day?

Day 5

- Did I notice any resistance to the sound or stillness today?
- What helped me stay present with the mantra?
- How is chanting different from other mindfulness practices I've tried?

Day 6

- What mantra or word have I returned to most often this week?
- How has the sound shaped my internal landscape?
- What feels sacred about this practice now?

Day 7

- What has this practice revealed about my relationship to sound and stillness?
- How has the repetition of sacred or intentional words shifted my emotional state?
- Did I experience moments of connection, clarity, or peace?
- How might I continue chanting—or integrate it into other practices?
- What will I carry forward from this week?

12

SACRED MOVEMENT (INSPIRED BY SUFISM / WHIRLING DERVISHES)

Dance, when you're broken open. Dance, if you've torn the bandage off. Dance in the middle of the fighting.

— RUMI

Movement can be a path to transcendence. In the Sufi tradition, the ritual of *sema* (the whirling dance of the Mevlevi dervishes) is a form of moving prayer. As the dervish spins, they seek to leave the ego behind and merge with the Divine. It is not performance; it is surrender. Sacred movement invites us to express what words cannot. It awakens the body, softens the heart, and allows the spirit to rise.

Sufi mystics developed the whirling ceremony as a form of spiritual devotion. In the *sema*, the dervish turns around a still axis, one hand reaching up to the heavens, the other turned toward the earth. The positioning of the body was to symbolize the soul's journey between worlds. The spinning reflected cosmic order: the movement of the planets, the circling of prayer, the turning of love around the Divine.*

Even outside the Sufi context, sacred movement is found in many traditions, including Hindu *tandava*, Christian liturgical dance, Indigenous trance dance, and modern practices such as yoga and ecstatic dance. These embodied rituals remind us that prayer doesn't always need stillness. Sometimes, the most profound stillness is found in motion.

Weekly Practice: Sacred Movement

This week, let your body become a prayer. You don't need to whirl like a dervish—move with presence and heart.

INSTRUCTIONS:

1. Choose gentle, instrumental, or devotional music that speaks to you.
2. Stand tall, close your eyes, and take a few grounding breaths.
3. Begin to move—slowly, intuitively. Let your body lead.
4. If you feel called, try spinning gently with your arms outstretched. Keep your center soft.
5. Let your movement become a wordless offering of joy, grief, longing, or devotion.
6. End by placing your hands over your heart and standing still in gratitude.

Sacred movement is one of the greatest instruments that teaches us the body is not separate from spirit. Whether you danced in joy or trembled in stillness, your body offered something true. And in that

---

* "Mevleviyah," *Encyclopedia Britannica*, accessed July 17, 2025, https://www.britannica.com/topic/Mevleviyah.

offering, something opened. Something turned. Something remembered how to pray.

Reflection Journal

D̲a̲y̲ ̲1̲

- How did it feel to move with intention today?
- Was there a moment when the movement felt sacred?
- What emotions surfaced?

_____
_____
_____
_____
_____
_____
_____
_____

D̲a̲y̲ ̲2̲

- Did I feel more connected to my body, breath, or spirit today?
- What kind of movement came naturally to me?
- How did I end the session—calmer, lighter, more present?

_____
_____
_____

Day 3

- Was it difficult or freeing to let go and move intuitively?
- What kind of music or silence helped open me up?
- Did I feel more grounded or expanded afterward?

Day 4

- What intention did I bring into my movement today?
- Did I notice any resistance, self-consciousness, or joy?
- What felt sacred in this practice?

Day 5

- Did I try spinning or turning today? How did it feel?
- Was there a sense of rhythm or flow that emerged?
- What did my body express that my words could not?

Day 6

- What shifts have I noticed in my energy, mood, or awareness?
- Did the movement feel like a form of prayer, healing, or release?
- What part of this practice has been most meaningful?

Day 7

- How has this practice changed my relationship to my body?
- Did I experience any moments of transcendence, peace, or connection?
- What emotions or memories came up through movement this week?
- How might I bring more movement into my spiritual life?
- What did I offer—and what did I receive?

13

SACRED FIRE RITUAL (INSPIRED BY NATIVE AMERICAN TRADITIONS)

I saw the sacred hoop of my people was one of many hoops that made one circle, wide as daylight and as starlight.

— BLACK ELK

Fire has long been honored as a sacred symbol of transformation, illumination, and purification. The flame becomes a bridge between the seen and unseen, the self and the Creator. In many Native American traditions, fire is used in prayer and ceremony to release burdens, connect with Spirit, and renew the heart's direction. In the glow of sacred fire, we remember our place in that circle. We remember that letting go is not destruction—it's renewal.

For many Indigenous communities, including the Lakota, Navajo, and Apache, fire is not just a tool; it is alive. Fire is central to sweat lodge rituals, pipe ceremonies, and other sacred gatherings. It is treated with reverence, as a messenger that carries human prayers to Spirit.* The fire is fed, honored, and never taken for granted.

It's essential to recognize that many Native American fire ceremonies are deeply rooted in specific tribal cultures, languages, and teachings. **These should not be copied or imitated without guidance and permission.** However, those outside these traditions can still approach fire with respect, as a symbol of release, purification, and intention. Even a simple candle, used mindfully, can become a sacred flame.

Weekly Practice: Sacred Fire Ritual

This week, use a candle each day as a symbol for release and renewal. Let it be your teacher in the art of letting go.
Instructions:

1. Place a small candle on a safe, steady surface.
2. Sit quietly with your eyes open or closed. Hold in your mind a thought, burden, or emotion you're ready to release.
3. Imagine placing that worry into the flame—not to destroy, but to transform.
4. Watch the flame as it burns. Let your breath slow. Let your grip loosen.
5. End with a word or prayer of gratitude for the chance to begin again.

Like fire, you are capable of transformation. You can burn away what no longer serves you for goodness, wholeness, and you rise lighter, clearer, and more rooted in truth. The flame does not just destroy; it illuminates. When you choose to let go, you make space for something new. That, too, is a sacred offering.

---

* Black Elk, *The Sacred Pipe: Black Elk's Account of the Seven Rites of the Oglala Sioux*, ed. Joseph Epes Brown (Norman: University of Oklahoma Press, 1989), 7–9.

Reflection Journal

Day 1

- What did I choose to release today?
- How did it feel to imagine the flame receiving it?
- What emotions came up during or after the ritual?

_____
_____
_____
_____
_____
_____
_____
_____
_____

Day 2

- Was it hard to let go today? Why or why not?
- What did the flame seem to symbolize or reflect on yourself?
- Did I feel any shift—physically, emotionally, or spiritually?

_____
_____
_____
_____

Day 3

- What does this flame represent to me now, midweek?
- Is there a burden I'm holding on to more tightly than I realized?
- What might it mean to release it fully?

Day 4

- Did today's practice feel different from earlier in the week?
- Was there peace, resistance, relief, or something else?
- What would it look like to carry the fire's clarity into my daily life?

Day 5

- What memory, thought, or emotion arose during today's ritual?
- What might this fire be teaching me about trust or surrender?
- How can I honor what I've let go of?

Day 6

- What patterns do I see in what I've chosen to release this week?
- Have I created any new space within myself?

- What might that space be for?

Day 7

- What have I learned about myself through the practice of symbolic release?
- How did the fire become a mirror for my inner world?
- What resistance did I meet this week, and what softened?
- In what ways did this practice renew my spirit or shift my perspective?
- What sacred fire will I carry forward?

14

SILENCE RETREAT (INSPIRED BY CHRISTIAN DESERT FATHERS)

Go, sit in your cell, and your cell will teach you everything.

—ABBA MOSES

Around the fourth century, a wave of men and women retreated into the deserts of Egypt, Syria, and Palestine. They were not looking to escape the world, but to meet God more intimately within the world. These Desert Fathers and Mothers lived in stillness, practicing silence as a way to listen, not just with their ears, but with their souls. In our noisy and overconnected world, silence is a rare medicine. It asks nothing and offers everything. It is an ancient spiritual tool for grounding, listening, and beginning again.

The Desert Fathers and Mothers are early Christian mystics who sought solitude as a path to transformation. In silence, they came face to face with their own thoughts, temptations, and insights. It is in silence they encountered the Divine. Their "cells" were not prisons but sanctuaries; simple spaces where silence became the teacher.*

The tradition of contemplative silence finds echoes in other spiritual paths. Buddhist monks, Taoist sages, and Indigenous seekers on vision quests have all turned to silence as a gateway to wisdom.† Stillness is not exclusive to one tradition; it is a universal path back to the voice within you.

Weekly Practice: Silence Retreat

This week, you're invited to carve out one hour for silence. Let it be a sacred appointment with your soul.

Instructions:

1. Select a quiet, undisturbed location (indoors or outdoors).
2. Set a timer for one hour. Leave your phone out of reach.
3. Do not speak, read, write, or listen to music. Just be.
4. You may sit still, walk slowly, or lie down, but stay present.
5. Notice what arises in the silence. You don't need to chase it or judge it.
6. Let the stillness shape you.

Silence is not emptiness. It is being present, waiting patiently beneath the noise. When you sit in the quiet long enough, your soul begins to speak; not with words, but with knowing. Let this stillness shape you, soften you, and bring you back to what's real.

---

* Thomas Merton, *The Wisdom of the Desert: Sayings from the Desert Fathers of the Fourth Century* (New York: New Directions, 1960), ix–xiii.
† Mirabai Starr, *God of Love: A Guide to the Heart of Judaism, Christianity, and Islam* (Rhinebeck, NY: Monkfish Book Publishing, 2012), 85–88.

Reflective Journal

Day 1

- What was most difficult about today's silence?
- What thoughts or emotions came up?
- Did I experience any moments of peace or clarity?

_____
_____
_____
_____
_____
_____
_____
_____
_____

Day 2

- How did I prepare myself to enter silence today?
- Did the silence feel empty, full, or something else?
- What did I learn about myself in this hour?

_____
_____
_____
_____
_____
_____
_____
_____
_____

Day 3

- What distractions or inner noise did I notice?
- Was there a moment when I felt deeply present?
- How do I feel now, after this practice?

_____
_____
_____
_____
_____
_____
_____
_____

Day 4

- Did the silence feel different from previous days?
- What surfaced that surprised me—emotionally, spiritually, or physically?
- What truth or insight did I sense in the quiet?

_____
_____
_____
_____
_____
_____
_____
_____

Day 5

- Was today's silence comforting or uncomfortable?
- Did any recurring thoughts or patterns appear?
- How am I beginning to relate to silence?

Day 6

- What gifts has the silence offered me so far?
- How has my mind or heart shifted this week?
- What feels sacred about this practice now?

Day 7

- How did this week of silence affect my emotional, mental, or spiritual state?
- What did I resist—and what did I welcome—in the stillness?
- Did any deep truth, insight, or question arise during this retreat?
- How might I return to silence more regularly in my life?
- What part of me feels renewed, rested, or more whole?

15

BLESSING FOOD (INSPIRED BY JUDAISM)

When you have eaten and are satisfied, bless the LORD your God for the good land he has given you.

— DEUTERONOMY 8:10; NIV

The practice of blessing food (before or after a meal) turns something ordinary into something sacred. In Judaism, this practice is known as *Birkat Hamazon* (grace after meals) and it is rooted in the deep awareness that all nourishment is a gift. This moment of blessing invites us to slow down, offer thanks, and reconnect with the Source of all life. Gratitude, when woven into something as simple as a meal, becomes a way of life.

In Jewish tradition, meals are framed by blessings: one before eating (*berachot*) and one afterward (*Birkat Hamazon*). These rituals aren't only about food, they're about mindfulness, memory, and reverence. Every meal becomes a moment to thank the Creator, the land, and the hands that made it possible.*

---

* Ronald H. Isaacs, *Every Person's Guide to Jewish Prayer* (Northvale, NJ: Jason Aronson, 1997), 77–79.

This custom echoes across cultures and faiths. In Islam, meals typically begin with the phrase *bismillah* (In the name of God). In Christianity, people often say grace. Indigenous traditions usually involve offering food to ancestors or spirit beings before partaking. Blessing food is one of the oldest forms of embodied gratitude.

Weekly Practice: Food Blessing

This week, transform your meals into moments of sacred connection. Bless your food before and after eating (formally or informally, silently or aloud).

INSTRUCTIONS:

1. Before eating, pause and take one slow, mindful breath.
2. Offer a simple word or phrase of gratitude (e.g., "Thank you for this nourishment," or "Blessed are You, Source of Life").
3. As you eat, stay aware of the texture, taste, and effort that brought the food to your table.
4. After eating, take a moment to offer thanks to the earth, the growers, the animals or plants, and the unseen web of life that sustains you.

To bless your food is to bless your life. With every bite, you have a chance to say thank you for the earth, for labor, for breath, for being alive. Gratitude isn't just a feeling; it is a practice. And this practice can turn any meal into communion with the sacred.

Reflective Journal

Day 1

- What did I bless before my meal today?
- How did this small ritual affect my mood or awareness?
- Did anything about the food feel different when blessed?

_____
_____
_____
_____
_____
_____
_____
_____

Day 2

- Did I remember to bless my food before eating? Why or why not?
- What feelings or memories came up as I gave thanks?
- Did this effect how much or how quickly I ate?

_____
_____
_____
_____
_____
_____
_____
_____

Day 3

- What do I normally take for granted about food and eating?
- How did today's blessing help me remember something deeper?
- Did I notice any sense of connection with the land or people?

_____
_____
_____
_____
_____
_____
_____
_____

Day 4

- Was today's blessing spontaneous or structured?
- Did it feel meaningful or mechanical—and why?
- How did I feel physically and emotionally after the meal?

_____
_____
_____
_____
_____
_____
_____
_____

Day 5

- Who or what did I silently include in my blessing today?
- Did this act help shift my attention toward gratitude or presence?
- What does "spiritual nourishment" mean to me?

Day 6

- What was the most nourishing part of today's meal—beyond the food?
- How have these blessings affected my relationship with daily routines?
- What would it look like to eat with reverence every day?

DAY 7.

- What did I learn about gratitude through this week's practice?
- How did blessing meals affect my sense of connection—to God, the earth, or others?
- Did this practice create more presence or joy in daily life?
- What intention do I want to carry forward into how I eat, give thanks, and receive nourishment?

16
THE FOUR DIRECTIONS (INSPIRED BY INDIGENOUS NORTH AMERICA)

Everything the power of the world does is done in a circle.

— BLACK ELK

Many Native American traditions honor the four directions (East, South, West, and North) as sacred. Each holds its wisdom, representing various aspects of life, elements of nature, and teachings on balance. When we turn to the directions with intention, we remember our place in the great circle of life. The Four Directions are not just compass points. They are teachers. When you pause to honor them (even briefly) your spirit realigns with something ancient, grounding, and whole.

The Four Directions appear in spiritual teachings across many Indigenous nations, including Lakota, Ojibwe, Navajo, and Cherokee communities.* Each direction can symbolize a stage of life (birth, youth, adulthood, elderhood), a season, an element, or a sacred color.

---

* Michael Tlanusta Garrett, *Walking on the Wind: Cherokee Teachings for Harmony and Balance* (Rochester, VT: Bear & Company, 1998), 15–23.

While meanings vary among tribes, the core teaching is shared: everything is interconnected.

The Medicine Wheel is one expression of this sacred circle. It is used in prayer, storytelling, and healing ceremonies as a map of harmony, showing how all things live about one another: people, animals, elements, ancestors, and Spirit.[*]

While it is important not to replicate these ceremonial practices, you can engage with these teachings respectfully by learning, listening, and honoring the values of gratitude, balance, and respect for all beings.

Weekly Practice: Greeting the Four Directions

This week, create a simple ritual of greeting the Four Directions to bring groundedness and sacred presence into your day.

INSTRUCTIONS:

1. Stand outside with a clear sense of direction. If indoors, imagine the directions around you.
2. Begin facing East. Breathe deeply and say: "Thank you for new beginnings."
3. Turn to the South. Say: "Thank you for growth and warmth."
4. Face West. Say: "Thank you for rest and reflection."
5. Face North. Say: "Thank you for wisdom and strength."
6. Close with a deep breath and silently acknowledge your place in the circle of life.

The Four Directions invite you into a deeper relationship with the world around you. In honoring the East, South, West, and North, you

---

[*] Native Land Digital, "Resources on Indigenous Knowledge and Land Acknowledgment," accessed July 17, 2025, https://native-land.ca/resources/.

are remembering that you live in a circle of connection. A circle where all beings matter, and where your life has meaning.

Reflection Journal

Day 1

- Which direction felt most resonant to me today?
- What emotion or memory came up as I turned?
- Did this practice help me feel more connected to the earth or myself?

_____
_____
_____
_____
_____
_____
_____
_____

Day 2

- How did I feel before and after the practice?
- Was there a sense of grounding, or did it feel unfamiliar?
- What direction might represent what I need right now?

_____
_____
_____

Day 3

- Did I notice anything in nature or my body during this ritual?
- What would it mean to walk through the day in harmony with the directions?
- How do I understand "sacred space" after today?

Day 4

- Which direction felt difficult or distant today? Why?
- What might that direction be asking me to learn or remember?
- How can I bring this awareness into my relationships?

Day 5

- Did the ritual feel like a form of prayer or meditation?
- What did the circle teach me about balance or wholeness today?
- Was there a moment of clarity, gratitude, or stillness?

Day 6

- Has my relationship with the land or sky shifted this week?

- What patterns have I noticed in my thoughts, emotions, or energy?
- What new beginnings or completions are present in my life?

Day 7

- What did the Four Directions awaken or remind me of?
- How has this simple daily turning affected my sense of spiritual orientation?
- What do I now see as sacred that I may have overlooked before?
- What does it mean to walk in balance with the natural world?

17

TEA CEREMONY (INSPIRED BY JAPANESE ZEN)

Tea is a religion of the art of life.

— OKAKURA KAKUZŌ

Ordinary acts can become sacred when we slow down and bring our presence to them. In Japanese Zen culture, the tea ceremony (*chanoyu*) transforms the act of preparing and serving tea into a serene ritual of mindfulness, grace, and gratitude. It's not about the tea; it's about how we serve, how we receive, and how we *show up*. When we move slowly, with intention, even a single cup of tea can become a doorway into stillness and spiritual awareness.

The Japanese tea ceremony was shaped over centuries by Zen Buddhist principles that values harmony (*wa*), respect (*kei*), purity (*sei*), and tranquility (*jaku*). Rooted in the aesthetics of simplicity and imperfection (*wabi-sabi*), this tradition invites us to be fully present with what is.

While elaborate formal ceremonies exist, even a quiet moment alone with a cup of tea can honor the same spirit.* By noticing the heat of the water, the feel of the cup, and the silence between sips, we reawaken to the beauty of what's right in front of us.

Weekly Practice: Tea Ceremony

This week, treat your tea as a daily meditation—whether you use matcha, herbal tea, or your favorite mug of morning warmth.

INSTRUCTIONS:

1. Set aside a few quiet minutes each day.
2. Prepare your tea slowly, paying attention to each step (boiling the water, selecting your cup, and steeping the leaves).
3. Before drinking, pause. Offer gratitude for the water, the leaves, and the people who grew and harvested them.
4. Drink slowly, in silence if possible. Notice the warmth, aroma, and taste.
5. When finished, clean your space with the same reverence and care.

When you prepare and serve tea with awareness, you're not just making a drink—you're practicing how to live. In the quiet of a simple cup, you may discover a spaciousness that can ripple into every part of your day.

---

* "The Japanese Way of Tea," Urasenke Foundation, accessed July 17, 2025, https://urasenke.or.jp/texte/tea_2.html

Reflection Journal

Day 1

- What kind of tea did I prepare today?
- How did I feel as I moved through the ritual?
- Was there a moment when I felt more still or aware?

_____
_____
_____
_____
_____
_____
_____
_____
_____

Day 2

- Did I feel rushed, or was I able to slow down?
- What details did I notice about the tea or the setting?
- How did this moment affect the rest of my day?

_____
_____
_____
_____
_____
_____

Day 3

- Did I treat the preparation and cleanup with the same presence?
- What surprised me about today's tea ritual?
- Did anything feel different in my body or mind?

Day 4

- How did I respond to silence during the tea ritual?
- What emotions arose, if any?
- What small details made this practice feel sacred?

Day 5

- Did I find beauty in something I'd normally overlook?
- What does "ritual" mean to me after this practice?
- How might I bring this kind of presence into other routines?

Day 6

- What did the tea ritual teach me about mindfulness today?
- Did I feel more connected to myself or to the natural world?
- Is there a metaphor or insight I want to carry forward?

DAY 7

- What did I discover by turning tea into a ritual?
- How has this practice changed my relationship with everyday actions?
- What deeper values (like care, reverence, or slowness) did I reconnect with?
- In what other areas of life might I bring this mindful attention?

18
SUNRISE RENEWAL (INSPIRED BY PAGAN AND NEO-PAGAN TRADITIONS)

Every dawn holds the promise of transformation.

— STARHAWK

The sunrise is one of the world's oldest prayers. Across cultures, the rising sun is a symbol of hope, rebirth, and divine presence. In Pagan and Neo-Pagan traditions, greeting the dawn is a spiritual act as an invitation to begin anew and align with the natural cycles. Whether you follow a Pagan path or are seeking renewal, watching the sunrise can open the heart to possibility, gratitude, and gentle power.

Ancient Pagan cultures honored the sun as sacred, often aligning their rituals with celestial events such as the solstices and equinoxes. In modern Neo-Pagan and Wiccan practice, sunrise rituals serve to welcome the light, affirm intentions, and celebrate connection to the earth's rhythms.* These practices don't require elaborate altars or festivals. It only requires your presence. Greeting the dawn with

---

* Odeen, "Pagan Sunrise Rituals," *Patheos Pagan*, accessed July 17, 2025, https://www.patheos.com/blogs/oedenshore/2021/06/pagan-sunrise-rituals/.

breath, prayer, movement, or silence becomes a spiritual rhythm. The act itself is the offering.

Weekly Practice: Sunrise Renewal

This week, greet the sunrise as a ritual of renewal.

INSTRUCTIONS:

1. Set an alarm to rise just before sunrise.
2. Step outside or sit near a window facing east.
3. As the light changes, take slow, deep breaths.
4. Offer a simple phrase or prayer (e.g., "I welcome this new day" or "Let this light guide me").
5. Reflect quietly or journal afterward if time allows.

Every sunrise offers a quiet miracle: a fresh beginning, a soft reset, a return to light. Whether you rise in silence or with song, the dawn of a new day invites your spirit to awaken alongside the world.

Reflection Journal

DAY 1

- What did the sky look like when I greeted the sunrise?
- How did it feel to begin my day with intention?
- What is one hope I'm carrying into this new day?

_____
_____
_____
_____

Day 2

- Did anything shift in my mood or energy afterward?
- What thoughts or emotions came up in the silence?
- What word or image stayed with me from the sunrise?

Day 3

- Was it difficult to slow down this morning? Why or why not?
- How did this moment connect me to nature or spirit?
- Did I feel any resistance to beginning again?

Day 4

- What did I notice in my body as I welcomed the light?
- What intention rose up for me today?
- Is there something I need to release to make space for renewal?

Day 5

- How has watching the sunrise affected my sense of time or pace?
- What lessons does the sunrise offer about change or consistency?

- How can I carry this energy with me into busy moments?

Day 6

- What has surprised me most about this week's practice?
- Have I found a personal rhythm or ritual in the morning?
- What does the sunrise symbolize in my own spiritual life?

Day 7

- How has greeting the sunrise shaped my mornings or mindset?
- What did I learn about myself by showing up each day?
- Did I feel more attuned to the rhythms of nature or spirit?
- How might I create a lasting ritual from this experience?

_____
_____
_____
_____
_____
_____
_____
_____
_____
_____
_____
_____
_____
_____
_____
_____
_____
_____
_____
_____
_____
_____
_____
_____
_____
_____

19

THE ROSARY (INSPIRED BY CATHOLIC CHRISTIANITY)

The Rosary, though clearly Marian in character, is at heart a Christocentric prayer.

— POPE JOHN PAUL II

There is something powerful about repetition, it quiets the noise and brings the soul into rhythm. In Catholic tradition, the Rosary is a meditative prayer that combines physical movement, breath, and sacred words. It helps the heart focus, opens the spirit to grace, and allows space for stillness to grow. Whether or not you identify with the Catholic faith, the practice of repeated prayer on beads can offer a grounding rhythm and a sense of inner peace.

The Rosary, as we know it, developed during the Middle Ages as a way for laypeople to meditate on the life of Christ through a structured, rhythmic prayer. Traditionally, the devotion includes the *Our Father*, repeated *Hail Marys*, and reflections on sacred *mysteries*.

The use of beads or physical counters for prayer isn't exclusive to Catholicism. Hindu *japa mala*, Islamic *misbaha*, and Buddhist prayer beads all serve similar purposes: to calm the mind, align the breath with intention, and foster spiritual connection through repetition.

Weekly Practice: The "Rosay"

This week, try a simple meditative prayer using a word or phrase and a set of beads or counters.

Instructions:

1. Choose a calming word or phrase (e.g., "peace," "mercy," "I am held").
2. Find or create a set of beads, stones, or knots (10 is a good starting number).
3. Sit comfortably and slowly repeat the word, moving your fingers along each bead.
4. Allow yourself to fall into the rhythm. If your mind wanders, return to the repetition.

Repetition can be a doorway to peace. Like the steady beat of a drum or the rhythm of breath, the Rosary invites us into a more profound stillness, one that speaks not through words, but through the quiet of the heart.

Reflection Journal

Day 1

- What word or phrase did you choose today?
- How did it feel to repeat it slowly with each breath or bead?
- Did your mind resist or relax?

Day 2

- Was there a moment during the practice that felt meaningful or quieting?
- How did your body respond to the repetition?
- Did any emotions arise?

Day 3

- Did the repetition help anchor your focus?
- What images or thoughts came to mind as you prayed?

- Would you like to try a different word tomorrow?

Day 4

- Was it easier or harder to stay present today?
- How does this practice compare to silent meditation or other forms of prayer?
- Are you noticing any changes in your energy or attitude?

Day 5

- Did the act of using beads or counters help you feel more grounded?
- How did you carry the energy of this practice into the rest of your day?
- What does this repetition remind you of in other areas of life?

_____
_____
_____
_____
_____
_____
_____

Day 6

- What did you learn about your mind or heart this week through repetition?
- Did anything shift in how you view prayer or meditation?
- What has felt most meaningful so far?

_____
_____
_____
_____
_____

Day 7

- What did you discover through repeating a sacred word or phrase?
- How did the use of beads or tactile counters influence your experience?
- Did this practice bring you closer to peace, faith, or inner stillness in any way?
- Could this be something you return to in times of stress or transition?

20

DREAM JOURNALING (INSPIRED BY GREEK PHILOSOPHY / ASCLEPIAN TRADITION)

I knew that dreams were more than illusions. They were the means through which the gods cared for me.

— AELIUS ARISTIDES

For thousands of years, dreams have been honored as sacred messages, windows into the unconscious, the soul, or the divine. In ancient Greece, seekers would visit healing temples dedicated to Asclepius, the god of medicine, to receive guidance through dreams. The dreams were not seen as mere stories of the night; they were conversations with the sacred. Keeping a dream journal allows you to begin noticing the subtle guidance your dreams may offer and opens the door to deeper self-awareness.

The practice of dream incubation (*enkoimesis*) was central to ancient Asclepian healing. Pilgrims would undergo ritual purification and then sleep in a sacred chamber, hoping to receive a dream that would diagnose or heal their condition. Upon waking, they would share their dreams with temple priests, who would offer interpretations and prescribe remedies.

This tradition is not unique to ancient Greece. Indigenous

communities, mystics, and spiritual teachers across cultures have honored dreams as sources of divine insight, like the dreams of Joseph in the Hebrew Bible or the vision quests of Native American traditions.* Today, psychologists like Carl Jung echoed this view, suggesting that dreams reveal hidden parts of us longing to be integrated.

Weekly Practice

This week, you'll begin a simple dream journaling practice. Even if your dreams seem scattered or unclear, the act of writing them down build's awareness over time.

Instructions:

1. Keep *Awaken* and a pen beside your bed.
2. Upon waking (before checking your phone or getting out of bed) write down everything you remember, even fragments, emotions, or images.
3. If you don't remember a dream, note that too, and write a simple intention for the next night.
4. Reflect: Is there a feeling, message, or metaphor present? What might your inner wisdom be trying to say?

Your dreams may be more than random images, they may be subtle messengers offering wisdom, healing, or clarity. By making space for them, you open yourself to a quieter, deeper voice within.

---

* "Dream Incubation in Ancient Greek Temples," *Ancient Origins*, https://www.ancient-origins.net/history-ancient-traditions/dream-incubation-0014215.

Reflection Journal

Day 1

- What do you remember from your dream(s)?
- How did it feel—peaceful, confusing, vivid, foggy?
- Is there a word, symbol, or message that stands out?

_____
_____
_____
_____
_____
_____
_____
_____

Day 2

- Was your dream connected to anything from your waking life?
- Did any patterns, people, or places appear again?
- What emotions lingered after waking?

_____
_____
_____
_____
_____
_____

Day 3

- What was the overall energy of your dream: light, dark, strange, comforting?
- Are there any metaphors or symbols that speak to you?
- If this dream had a title, what would it be?

Day 4

- Did anything shift in your dream clarity or recall today?
- What part of the dream felt most significant?
- Was there a moment that felt healing or challenging?

Day 5

- Do you sense any recurring themes over the past few days?
- Is your subconscious trying to tell you something?
- How does this dream reflect your current state of being?

Day 6

- What surprised you about your dream last night?
- What part of the dream are you still thinking about?
- If this dream offered advice, what would it be?

Day 7

- What themes or symbols appeared most often?
- Did your awareness of your dreams improve throughout the week?
- What personal insight, if any, came through this practice?
- How might you continue working with dreams as a spiritual or emotional tool?

21

CANDLE GAZING (INSPIRED BY TRATAKA, YOGA)

Trataka eradicates all diseases of the eyes, fatigue and sloth, and brings about clairvoyance.

— HATHA YOGA PRADIPIKA 2.32

Sometimes, the simplest practices offer the deepest calm. In the yogic tradition, Trataka is a focused gazing meditation using a candle flame. Practiced in darkness and stillness, it's a way of training both the outer eyes and the inner vision, strengthening concentration, steadying the mind, and awakening insight.

Trataka is one of the six classical purification techniques (*shatkarmas*) found in the *Hatha Yoga Pradipika*, a foundational 15th-century Sanskrit text on yoga. Traditionally, this practice is said to stimulate the *ajna chakra*, also known as the "third eye," which represents intuition and inner knowing.

Modern yogic teachers, such as Swami Satyananda Saraswati, have incorporated this technique into contemporary practice, framing it as both a concentration aid and a doorway into meditative stillness. While it originates from a Hindu yogic lineage, the act of gazing at a flame in silence is a cross-cultural symbol of spiritual focus, found in Christian vigils, Buddhist lamp offerings, and other traditions. You don't need to believe in esoteric powers to benefit. Sitting quietly with a candle can become a sacred moment of presence, light, and inward clarity.

Weekly Practice: Candle Gazing

This week, you'll engage in candle gazing as a meditative ritual. It is a short practice that can be done in the early morning or evening.
Instructions:

1. Sit in a quiet, dark room with minimal distractions.
2. Place a candle on a stable surface at eye level, about 2–3 feet away.
3. Light the candle and sit comfortably, with your spine upright.
4. Gaze at the tip of the flame without blinking for 1–2 minutes.
5. Close your eyes and observe the inner afterimage in your mind's eye.
6. When it fades, repeat the cycle 2–3 more times.
7. Finish with a few slow breaths in the dark.

A single flame in the dark can become a doorway to stillness, vision, and clarity. Through Trataka, you practice seeing with more than just your eyes; you learn to look within.

Reflection Journal

Day 1

- How did it feel to sit still and gaze at the flame?
- Did your mind resist or settle?
- What did you notice in your body?

_____
_____
_____
_____
_____
_____
_____
_____

Day 2

- Was it easier to keep your gaze today?
- Did any inner images or colors appear after closing your eyes?
- How did your mind feel afterward?

_____
_____
_____
_____
_____

Day 3

- Was it difficult not to blink or move?
- Did the candlelight bring a sense of comfort or challenge?
- What emotions arose during or after the practice?

Day 4

- What changes have you noticed in your focus or attention?
- How long did the afterimage last today?
- How would you describe your inner state post-practice?

Day 5

- Did the flame feel symbolic or sacred to you today?
- Were you more aware of your breath, body, or mind?
- Any resistance or insight that came up?

Day 6

- Was today's practice different from earlier in the week?
- Did your mind wander less, more, or the same?
- What stands out to you about this technique so far?

Day 7

- Did this practice help quiet your mind or sharpen your focus?
- How did your relationship with stillness or light evolve this week?
- What, if anything, did this practice awaken or clarify in you?
- Will you continue this ritual moving forward?

22
SACRED STORYTELLING (INSPIRED BY WEST AFRICAN GRIOT TRADITION)

When a griot dies, it's as if a library has burned to the ground.

— *AMADOU HAMPÂTÉ BÂ*

Storytelling has always been more than entertainment; it's a vessel for truth, identity, and resilience. In West African cultures, griots serve as oral historians, musicians, and spiritual memory keepers, preserving the heartbeat of a people through storytelling and song. To tell a story is to pass on wisdom, to remember who you are, and to remind others they are not alone.

In countries such as Mali, Senegal, and Guinea, *griots* (or *jali* in the Manding languages) have served as keepers of lineage, praise singers, and counselors. They carry the ancestral memory of families and communities, often through spoken word and music. These sacred narratives aren't just historical; they are spiritual, offering guidance, connection, and healing. Storytelling as a holy act is found across cultures: in the teachings of Indigenous elders, in the parables of sacred texts, and family stories passed down through generations. The griot reminds us: your story matters. Sharing it is a gift.

Weekly Practice: Sacred Storytelling

Each day this week, connect to the power of your story. Instructions:

1. Reflect on a personal story that taught you something about strength, identity, or transformation.
2. Please write it down or speak it aloud.
3. Please share it with someone you trust or record it as a gift for future generations.

Your story is sacred. Telling it can be an offering to yourself, to your ancestors, and to those yet to come. In a world hungry for meaning, sharing our lived truth is a radical act of connection.

Reflection Journal

DAY 1

- What personal story came to mind today?
- How did it feel to begin telling it?
- What strength or insight does it carry?

_____
_____
_____
_____
_____
_____
_____

Day 2

- Was it easy or difficult to remember the details?
- Did telling your story bring up emotions?
- How did the listener (or your journal) receive it?

Day 3

- What values or lessons are embedded in this story?
- Have you ever shared this story before?
- What was different about telling it now?

Day 4

- How has this story shaped who you are today?
- What details or symbols stood out?
- Would you tell this story to someone younger than you?

_____
_____
_____
_____
_____
_____
_____
_____

Day 5

- What part of your story still feels unresolved?
- Is there something you're proud of in this story?
- How might this story help someone else?

_____
_____
_____
_____
_____
_____
_____
_____

Day 6

- How did it feel to revisit this memory again?
- Did writing or speaking it shift your perspective?
- What do you want to remember about this experience?

Day 7

- Which story did you explore most deeply this week?
- What healing, insight, or transformation came from telling it?
- What role does storytelling play in your spiritual resilience?

23

MINDFUL TOUCH (INSPIRED BY TAOIST QI GONG)

Where the mind goes, the qi flows.

— TAOIST TRADITION

Touch can be more than physical. Touch can be sacred. In Taoist energy practices, touch is used to guide *qi* (life force) through the body, releasing tension and restoring inner balance. When we place our hands on the body with presence and care, we are offering ourselves compassion, healing, and connection.

In classical Taoist medicine, *qi* is the subtle energy believed to animate life. Practices such as *Qi Gong* and mindful self-touch utilize breath, intention, and physical contact to move and nourish this energy. These techniques appear in ancient medical texts such as the *Huangdi Neijing* (The Yellow Emperor's Classic of Medicine), a foundational work in Traditional Chinese Medicine.[*]

While often taught in the context of healing arts, these practices are spiritual at heart. These practices have a way of bringing body,

---

[*] *Huangdi Neijing* (ca. 2nd century BCE), foundational text of Chinese medicine and Taoist energetics.

mind, and energy into harmony. Similar to Reiki in Japan or Christian laying-on-of-hands, mindful touch is a universal gesture of affirmation, presence, and love.

Weekly Practice: Mindful Touch

This week, use mindful touch as a healing ritual.

INSTRUCTIONS:

1. Find a quiet place and sit comfortably.
2. Rub your hands together slowly until they feel warm.
3. Place them gently over your heart, belly, or head.
4. Take a few deep breaths and imagine warm, healing energy flowing from your hands into that area.
5. If you like, repeat a kind word silently — "peace," "heal," or "love."

Your body is worthy of kindness. Through the gentle art of mindful touch, you return home to yourself one breath, one hand, one moment at a time.

Reflection Journal

Day 1

- What was it like to offer your body intentional touch today?
- Did it feel comforting, awkward, healing, or something else?
- Where did you notice tension or softness?

_____
_____
_____
_____
_____
_____
_____
_____

Day 2

- How did the warmth of your hands affect your awareness?
- Did any emotions surface during the practice?

_____
_____
_____
_____
_____

Day 3

- Which area of your body did you focus on today?
- What sensations or shifts did you observe?

Day 4

- Were you able to stay present during the practice, or did your mind wander?
- How did you gently return your focus?

Day 5

- What kind word or intention did you silently speak to your body today?
- How did that affect your mood or mindset?

Day 6

- In what ways did this practice feel different from simply resting or relaxing?
- Did it change your relationship to your body?

Day 7

- What patterns did you notice in how you respond to your own touch?
- Did this practice deepen your sense of connection, trust, or tenderness with your body?
- How might you integrate this kind of presence into your daily life beyond this week?

24

ACTS OF SERVICE (INSPIRED BY CHRISTIANITY/SIKHISM)

For even the Son of Man came not to be served but to serve.

— MARK 10:45

True service is love in action. When we serve others, not for praise, but with quiet humility, we step into a sacred stream that flows through many traditions. In Sikhism, *seva* (selfless service) is one of the highest expressions of devotion and equality. Whether it's washing dishes at a community kitchen or helping someone in need, service becomes a path toward spiritual liberation. When we give with a pure heart, we uplift others and become more whole ourselves.

The Sikh holy text, the Guru Granth Sahib, elevates *seva* as a core spiritual discipline. Service is seen as a way to dissolve our egos and connect with the Divine.* In Christianity, service is an imitation of Christ's love, a call to care for "the least of these" without seeking

---

* Pashaura Singh, *The Guru Granth Sahib: Canon, Meaning and Authority* (New York: Oxford University Press, 2000), 219.

recognition.* Both traditions affirm that even small acts of kindness have a ripple effect. Whether faith-based or not, many people experience a deep sense of purpose when they serve with love.

Weekly Practice: Acts of Service

Each day this week, perform one small act of service (preferably anonymously).

INSTRUCTIONS:

1. Look for ways to quietly help someone without expecting anything in return.
2. This could be paying for someone's meal, doing a chore without being asked, leaving a kind note, or listening deeply.
3. Offer the action inwardly as a spiritual gift—no recognition needed.

When you serve others with love, you participate in the sacred work of healing the world. Service transforms the ordinary into holy ground, reminding you that your hands, your time, and your heart can be instruments of grace.

---

* Ronald H. Isaacs, *Every Person's Guide to Jewish Prayer* (Northvale, NJ: Jason Aronson, 1997), 108.

Reflection Journal

Day 1

- What act of service did you offer today?
- How did it feel to give without receiving recognition?
- Did you notice any shift in your inner state?

_____
_____
_____
_____
_____
_____
_____
_____
_____

Day 2

- Was there a moment today when you could have served but didn't?
- What held you back?
- How might you respond differently next time?

_____
_____
_____
_____
_____

Day 3

- What surprised you about today's act of service?
- Did it reveal anything about your assumptions, habits, or emotions?

Day 4

- Did your service feel joyful, inconvenient, fulfilling—or a mix?
- What does this tell you about your relationship to help others?

Day 5

- Did anyone serve you today?
- What was it like to receive?
- How did it impact your sense of connection or gratitude?

Day 6

- Reflect on your motivations: Were you serving from love, duty, or guilt?
- How do you want to refine your intention moving forward?

Day 7

- What have you learned about the role of service in your spiritual life?
- How did giving—without expecting thanks—change you?
- Where in your daily routine can you make small acts of love and service part of your rhythm?

25
LABYRINTH WALKING (INSPIRED BY CHRISTIAN MYSTICISM/ PAGAN EUROPE)

Solvitur ambulando — it is solved by walking.

— *LATIN PROVERB*

A labyrinth is not a maze; it has no tricks, no dead ends, no wrong turns. It is a single path, winding inward toward the center, and then back out again. In this way, walking a labyrinth becomes a living metaphor for the spiritual journey: entering deeper into yourself, meeting mystery at the core, and emerging with clarity or peace. The act of walking becomes prayer and movement becomes meditation. From medieval cathedrals to ancient stone carvings in Europe, the labyrinth has long served as a sacred space for seekers. And today, it continues to offer a quiet path of healing, especially for those who prefer movement to stillness.

Labyrinths have appeared in sacred architecture for thousands of years. In Pagan Europe, spiral and circular labyrinths were carved into stone as symbols of the cosmos, life cycles, or the goddess. In Christian mysticism, the labyrinth was used as a symbolic pilgrimage path, particularly for those who were unable to travel to Jerusalem.* The labyrinth at Chartres Cathedral in France (built in the 13th century) is one of the most famous examples.†

Today, both Christians and Neopagans utilize labyrinths as meditative tools, offering a quiet, embodied way to reflect, pray, or process emotions. Unlike a maze designed to confuse, a labyrinth is designed to guide to the center. In this practice, it serves to guide you back to the center of yourself.

Weekly Practice: Labyrinth Walking

Each day this week, walk a labyrinth or trace one slowly with your finger.

INSTRUCTIONS:

1. If available, visit a physical labyrinth. If not, print or draw one on paper.
2. Begin with a breath. Set a quiet intention or question in your heart.
3. Walk (or trace) slowly and mindfully, noticing thoughts and feelings as they arise.
4. Pause in the center. Listen. Then return outward with awareness and gratitude.

The labyrinth teaches that the path to peace is not always a linear one. It winds, turns, and sometimes feels uncertain, yet it always leads you deeper into yourself and back into the world with a new perspective. Let each step this week remind you that even when life feels complex, clarity comes through movement and reflection.

---

* Lauren Artress, *Walking a Sacred Path: Rediscovering the Labyrinth as a Spiritual Practice* (New York: Riverhead Books, 2006), 18–20.
† Penelope Reed Doob, *The Idea of the Labyrinth from Classical Antiquity through the Middle Ages* (Ithaca, NY: Cornell University Press, 1990), 203.

Reflection Journal

Day 1

- What was your intention or question before walking today?
- Did any thoughts or emotions surface as you followed the path?
- What did you notice about your pace or breath?

_____
_____
_____
_____
_____
_____
_____
_____
_____
_____

Day 2

- Did anything feel different about walking inward vs. walking outward?
- Was the center of the labyrinth meaningful to you today?
- How did the experience impact your state of mind?

_____
_____
_____
_____
_____
_____

Day 3

- Where in your life do you feel lost or uncertain?
- Did today's walk mirror any of those inner twists and turns?
- What insight or feeling emerged?

Day 4

- Did you experience resistance, restlessness, or stillness while walking?
- What does your reaction tell you about your relationship to quiet or slowness?
- How did your body feel during and after the walk?

Day 5

- What distractions showed up in your mind today?
- Were you able to gently return your focus to the path?
- How does this reflect your everyday habits?

Day 6

- Think about the difference between a maze and a labyrinth.
- How does the idea of "no wrong turns" influence the way you view your life or spiritual path?
- Write a few sentences about what that means for you.

_____
_____
_____
_____
_____
_____
_____
_____

Day 7

- What have you learned about your inner journey through the practice of labyrinth walking?
- How did it feel to have a clear path—one that asked you only to keep going, one step at a time?
- What will you carry forward from this experience into other areas of your life?

_____
_____
_____
_____
_____

26

FASTING (INSPIRED BY ISLAM AND MULTIPLE TRADITIONS)

Fasting is a shield.

— SURAH AL-BAQARAH 2:183–184

Fasting is more than abstaining from food. It is a sacred reset. Across nearly every spiritual tradition, fasting is employed to refine the heart, cultivate self-discipline, and deepen one's awareness of the Divine. By consciously stepping away from a comfort or habit, we are reminded of how little we truly need and how much can be revealed in emptiness. Whether it's food, technology, or another attachment, choosing to fast mindfully becomes an invitation. An invitation to pause, to listen more closely, and to reconnect with what matters most.

Fasting has deep roots across world traditions. In Islam, it is most visibly practiced during the month of Ramadan, when Muslims abstain from food, drink, and other pleasures from dawn until sunset. However, fasting also appears in Christianity (especially during Lent), Judaism (*Yom Kippur* and other fast days), Buddhism (monastic food restrictions), Hinduism (*Ekadashi* or *Navratri*), and even Stoic philosophy, which praised voluntary discomfort as a means of cultivating inner strength.* In all these paths, fasting is less about punishment and more about purification. Fasting is a way to create spiritual clarity by letting go of what distracts us.

Weekly Practice: Fasting

This week, choose a form of gentle, intentional fasting.

INSTRUCTIONS:

1. Choose a non-harmful fast: skip one meal, avoid sugar, or take a full-day break from screens or social media.
2. Before you begin each day, pause and set an intention for your fast.
3. When the urge to indulge arises, breathe. Return to your intention.
4. Use the space created by fasting for reflection, prayer, or quiet presence.
5. **Note:** This is not medical advice. If you are considering any food-related fast and have medical conditions, are pregnant, or are on medication, please consult with your doctor before beginning.

Fasting is not about denial. Fasting is about clarity. It clears away the excess and brings your attention back to what truly nourishes. Even small fasts can create sacred space for healing, insight, and freedom.

---

* William B. Irvine, *A Guide to the Good Life: The Ancient Art of Stoic Joy* (New York: Oxford University Press, 2009), 89–91.

Reflection Journal

Day 1

- What kind of fast did you choose today?
- How did your body and mind respond?
- What surprised you about the experience?

Day 2

- Did any emotions arise during the fast — restlessness, frustration, peace?
- What did those emotions teach you?
- Did you notice any habitual patterns or attachments?

Day 3

- How did it feel to interrupt your normal rhythm or routine?
- What space opened—mentally, spiritually, or emotionally?
- Write about what filled that space.

_____
_____
_____
_____
_____
_____
_____
_____
_____

Day 4

- Today, reflect on the idea of fasting as "a shield."
- What kinds of distractions or habits does fasting protect you from?
- How can it create space for insight or connection?

_____
_____
_____
_____
_____
_____

Day 5

- Was there any discomfort in today's practice?
- Instead of avoiding it, how did you meet it with compassion or awareness?
- Did anything shift?

Day 6

- Have you found any unexpected beauty or clarity during this week?
- What has fasting helped you see more clearly—about yourself or the world?
- Write about any inner transformation.

Day 7

- What did this week teach you about desire, sufficiency, and spiritual focus?
- Did your relationship with food, technology, or comfort shift in any way?
- How can you carry forward the practice of sacred restraint into your daily life?

27

FOREST BATHING (INSPIRED BY SHINRIN-YOKU, JAPAN)

The forest is the therapist.

— DR. QING LI

Sometimes healing doesn't require answers. It requires presence and awareness. In Japanese culture, *shinrin-yoku* (forest bathing) is the practice of immersing oneself in the quiet presence of trees. Not a hike, not a workout; it is about being, not doing. Simply standing among trees, letting your senses open, and receiving what the forest gives. This profound practice invites you to step out of stress and into a state of stillness. It reminds us that nature doesn't need to be fixed and neither do we.

Shinrin-yoku emerged in Japan during the 1980s as a response to rising rates of burnout and urban anxiety. Japanese scientists, particularly Dr. Qing Li, began studying the physiological effects of time spent in forests. Results showed measurable decreases in stress hormones (such as cortisol), lower blood pressure, improved immune function, and an elevated mood.*

Rooted in the Shinto appreciation of nature's sacredness, forest bathing echoes ancient practices found in many cultures —from Indigenous earth reverence to monastic walks in wooded cloisters. However, in modern life, it has become a counterbalance: a return to rhythm, rootedness, and breath.

Weekly Practice: Forest Bathing

This week, spend intentional time in nature (not for exercise) for presence.

INSTRUCTIONS:

1. Find a natural space with trees (i.e., a forest, park, or grove).
2. Leave your phone behind or on airplane mode.
3. Walk slowly and silently for 30–60 minutes.
4. Use your senses (smell the air, feel tree bark, listen to birds).
5. If you wish, sit on the ground and breathe gently. Let nature hold you.

The forest doesn't need you to be productive. It simply welcomes you. By slowing down in nature, you rediscover stillness, sensory connection, and you're belonging to the living world.

---

* Yoshifumi Miyazaki, *Shinrin Yoku: The Japanese Art of Forest Bathing* (London: Octopus Publishing, 2018).

Reflection Journal

Day 1

- Where did you go today for your forest walk?
- What did you notice with your senses—sight, sound, smell, touch?
- How did your body respond?

_____
_____
_____
_____
_____
_____
_____
_____

Day 2

- Was there a moment today when time seemed to slow down?
- What helped you be present?
- Write about anything that shifted in your mood or breath.

_____
_____
_____
_____
_____
_____
_____

Day 3

- Did you find any resistance to stillness today—boredom, restlessness, distraction?
- How did you respond?
- What did the forest seem to "say" in its quiet way?

Day 4

- Choose one tree to sit with or observe today.
- Describe it: bark, leaves, shape, scent, age, feeling.
- Did you sense any connection with it?

Day 5

- Were there any insights, emotions, or memories that came up during your time in nature today?
- Write freely, without judgment or analysis.

Day 6

- Return to a familiar spot.
- Did it feel different today? Did you?
- What layers of sound, light, or feeling emerged?

Day 7

- What have you learned about slowness, presence, and healing this week?
- Did this practice affect your stress, sleep, or overall sense of well-being?
- How might you keep a relationship with nature alive in your daily life?

28

BREATH OF FIRE (INSPIRED BY KUNDALINI YOGA)

The breath is the bridge between the body and the mind.

— YOGI BHAJAN

Breath of Fire is a rapid, rhythmic breathing technique used in Kundalini Yoga to awaken energy, build inner heat (*agni*), and clear mental fog. This breathwork activates the nervous system, improves oxygen flow, and produces resilience from the inside out. Breath of Fire is more than a technique. It is a practice of embodied awakening.

Breath of Fire (*Bhastrika* or *Agni Pran*) is central in Kundalini Yoga and some schools of classical Hatha Yoga. It is often used during *kriyas* (sets of physical and energetic exercises) to cultivate vitality, mental clarity, and spiritual focus. The breath is short, even, and continuous and is believed to stimulate the solar plexus, the energetic seat of willpower.

While Breath of Fire was popularized by Yogi Bhajan through Kundalini Yoga, variations of Breath of Fire have roots in ancient yogic texts, such as the Hatha Yoga Pradipika. Also, the practices have been integrated into modern breathwork and somatic therapies.*

Weekly Practice

This week, practice Breath of Fire daily to energize the body and focus the mind.

INSTRUCTIONS:

1. Sit comfortably with a straight spine. Close your eyes or focus softly on a point ahead.
2. Begin rapid, rhythmic breathing through the nose, short and equal inhales and exhales (about 2–3 per second).
3. Keep the breath light and even. The belly naturally expands and contracts.
4. Practice for 1 minute, then return to normal breathing and rest.
5. Gradually increase up to 3 minutes as you grow comfortable.
6. Note: This practice is not recommended for those who are pregnant, have high blood pressure, or suffer from respiratory or cardiovascular conditions. Always consult your healthcare provider before beginning new breathwork practices.

Breath is your inner fuel. When used with intention, it becomes a tool to ignite clarity, burn away distraction, and center you in your power. Breath of Fire reminds you that resilience begins from within you.

---

* Swami Muktibodhananda, *Hatha Yoga Pradipika* (Munger, Bihar, India: Bihar School of Yoga, 2002), 2.33.

Reflection Journal

<u>Day 1</u>

- What was my first impression of this breathing technique?
- Did I feel tension, resistance, or ease during the practice?
- How did my body respond in the minutes afterward?

_____
_____
_____
_____
_____
_____
_____
_____
_____

<u>Day 2</u>

- Was it easier or harder to maintain the rhythm today?
- Where in my body did, I feel the breath the most?
- Did I notice any emotional shifts after the session?

_____
_____
_____
_____
_____
_____
_____
_____
_____

Day 3

- What thoughts or distractions arose during the practice?
- Was I able to observe them without judgment?
- How did I return to the breath?

_____
_____
_____
_____
_____
_____
_____
_____

Day 4

- Did I feel more energized or calmer after today's session?
- How did this breathwork affect my focus during the day?
- What sensations stood out most?

_____
_____
_____
_____
_____
_____
_____
_____

Day 5

- Am I becoming more attuned to my body's energy?
- How does the concept of "inner fire" show up in my life today?
- What would it mean to channel this fire into something positive?

_____
_____
_____
_____
_____
_____
_____
_____
_____

Day 6

- What is one area in my life where I'd like to feel more clarity or strength?
- How might Breath of Fire support that intention?
- Is my breath becoming a bridge between mind and body?

_____
_____
_____
_____
_____
_____
_____
_____
_____

Day 7

- How has Breath of Fire changed my awareness of breath, energy, or emotion this week?
- In what ways did I experience discomfort, resistance, or growth?
- What have I learned about the connection between breath and resilience?
- Will I continue this practice? Why or why not?
- How might I integrate the power of breath more intentionally into my daily life?

29
SACRED GEOMETRY (INSPIRED BY PLATONIC PHILOSOPHY/ EGYPTIAN TEMPLES)

God geometrizes continually.

— *PLATO*

From the pyramids of Egypt to the spirals of Celtic art and the intricate mandalas of Hindu and Buddhist traditions, sacred geometry reflects the idea that specific shapes and patterns are more than just mathematical; they are the blueprint of the universe. The ancients believed these forms were the very language of creation. Circles, spirals, triangles, and other geometric figures were used not only in architecture and art but also in meditation and ritual. By working with these symbols, we are invited to experience harmony, beauty, and the hidden order of the cosmos.

Sacred geometry is found across cultures as a spiritual tool for connecting with the divine. In ancient Egypt, the triangle was used in pyramid construction to symbolize the connection between heaven and earth. In Vedic and Hindu traditions, yantras and mandalas are sacred visual tools that encode cosmic truths. In Neoplatonic philosophy, geometry was thought to reveal the structure of the soul and the divine order of being.

Patterns such as the golden ratio (φ), the flower of life, and spirals found in shells or galaxies have inspired spiritual reflection throughout history.* Contemplating these forms is not just an intellectual act. It is a meditative way to attune the mind to the harmony of creation.

Weekly Practice: Sacred Geometry

This week, engage with a sacred geometric form through meditation and drawing.

INSTRUCTIONS:

- Choose a shape (e.g., circle, spiral, triangle, seed of life).
- Quiet your space and take a few deep breaths.
- Slowly draw or trace the shape by hand.
- Gaze at it gently for a few minutes, letting it draw you inward.
- Reflect on its symbolism (i.e., wholeness, growth, harmony).
- Optional: Use it as a visual anchor during breathwork or silent prayer.

Sacred geometry reminds us of the beauty, balance, and spiritual truth are all around us. Even encoded into the shapes of life itself. By meditating on these patterns, we align ourselves with the deeper order of creation.

---

* Mario Livio, *The Golden Ratio: The Story of Phi, the World's Most Astonishing Number* (Broadway Books, 2003).

Reflection Journal

Day 1

- What shape did I choose to focus on today? Why was I drawn to it?
- How did I feel while drawing or observing it?
- Did any memories or emotions arise during the meditation?

_____
_____
_____
_____
_____
_____
_____

Day 2

- What deeper meaning might this shape hold in my current life?
- Did I notice any shifts in my mental or emotional state while focusing on it?
- What would it mean to see sacredness in design?

_____
_____
_____
_____

Day 3

- What symbols or patterns do I encounter regularly in daily life?
- Are there designs I once thought ordinary but now see as meaningful?
- How might I notice more hidden harmony around me?

Day 4

- Did I experience stillness or restlessness during today's practice?
- How did returning to the same shape (or a new one) feel?
- What insights, if any, arose from quiet contemplation?

Day 5

- Where do I feel a lack of balance or order in my life?
- How might sacred geometry help remind me of inner alignment?
- What qualities does this shape invite me to embody?

Day 6

- Have my feelings toward this practice shifted over the week?
- What spiritual or emotional resonance does this form now carry?
- If I imagined this shape representing part of my journey, what part would it be?

_____
_____
_____
_____
_____
_____
_____
_____
_____

Day 7

- How has contemplating sacred shapes changed the way I perceive the world around me?
- Did this practice help me cultivate more presence, peace, or inspiration?
- Will I continue to use visual symbols as a form of meditation or reflection? Why or why not?

_____
_____
_____
_____
_____

30

PURIFICATION WITH WATER
(INSPIRED BY SHINTO TRADITION)

Water is not just physical — it is spiritual. Flowing rivers, waterfalls, and even simple handwashing are seen as ways to realign oneself with nature and the divine.

— MOTOHISA YAMAKAGE

In Shinto, Japan's indigenous spirituality, purification is at the heart of sacred life. Known as misogi, the practice of ritual cleansing with water helps to remove spiritual impurities (*kegare*) and restore inner harmony (*ki*). When practiced mindfully, even a simple rinse of the hands can become a sacred act of renewal.

Misogi rituals range from full-body immersion in waterfalls or rivers to the more common practice of hand and mouth rinsing at Shinto shrines (*temizu*). These acts are not about moral guilt, but about energetic cleanliness and aligning one's spirit with the natural flow of the world and honoring the presence of *kami* (divine forces).

This practice is echoed in other traditions as well: Islamic *wudu* (ablutions), Jewish *netilat yadayim* (hand washing), and Christian holy water rituals all point to water as a sacred element of purification.

Weekly Practice: *Misogi*

Each day this week, engage in a water-based purification ritual.

INSTRUCTIONS:

1. Fill a small bowl with clean water or stand near running water.
2. Rinse your hands slowly, and if you wish, lightly touch the water to your face or chest.
3. As you do, say aloud or silently: *"May I be cleansed in body, heart, and spirit."*
4. Breathe deeply. Let the water carry away stress or negativity.
5. *Optional: If near a natural body of water, immerse your hands or feet as a deeper ritual of connection.*

With every intentional rinse or splash, you return to balance with yourself, with nature, and with the sacred. Let the simplicity of water cleanse not just your hands, but also your spirit.

Reflection Journal

Day 1

- What do I need to let go of today?
- How did the water feel on my skin?
- Did anything shift in my mood or energy afterward?

_____
_____
_____
_____
_____

Day 2

- Where do I carry spiritual or emotional "dirt"?
- How might I invite more simplicity into my inner life?
- What does purity mean to me — not as perfection, but as alignment?

Day 3

- What does water symbolize to me personally or culturally?
- Where in my life am I resisting flow?
- How can I soften and return to harmony?

Day 4

- Did this practice feel sacred or mechanical? Why?
- What did I notice in my body and breath during the ritual?
- What happens when I slow down even the smallest act?

Day 5

- What or who do I need to release with love today?
- In what ways am I renewing my energy and spirit this week?
- What did I learn about sacredness in ordinary things?

Day 6

- What in nature feels like "pure" energy to me?
- How does the idea of purification relate to self-care?
- What part of myself have I avoided that now wants attention?

Day 7

- How has this week changed my relationship to water?
- What do I want to carry forward from this practice?

- What does it mean to be "spiritually clean" in a messy world?

31

VISUALIZATION (INSPIRED BY TIBETAN BUDDHISM)

The image is not other than the mind; the mind is not other than the image.

— THE TIBETAN BOOK OF THE DEAD

In Tibetan Buddhism, visualization is not make-believe; it's a sacred training of the mind. Practitioners visualize enlightened beings or symbolic landscapes to cultivate compassion, courage, and clarity. Visualization can awaken your deepest qualities by focusing on what you aspire to become.

In Tibetan Buddhism, visualization plays a central role in many meditative practices, particularly in deity yoga. Practitioners may visualize themselves as *Avalokiteshvara* (the bodhisattva of compassion) or other enlightened beings, not as delusion, but as a method to dissolve ego and awaken buddha-nature.

This practice echoes other spiritual traditions too. Christian mystics meditated on scenes from the life of Christ, and Indigenous shamans visualize spirit helpers or power animals. Visualization can serve as a spiritual mirror, reflecting what is most sacred within you.

Weekly Practice

EACH DAY THIS WEEK, practice sacred visualization.

INSTRUCTIONS:

1. Sit comfortably with your spine upright and eyes closed.
2. Visualize a glowing sphere of light above your head.
3. Imagine this light representing peace, compassion, or strength.
4. Slowly visualize the light descending and filling your body.
5. Expand the light outward — to loved ones, your community, and the world.
6. End by resting in stillness and gratitude.

Your mind is a canvas, and visualization is how you paint it with peace. This sacred practice can rewire your inner world and ripple out into how you live, love, and serve.

Reflection Journal

Day 1

- What did I choose to visualize today?
- How did it affect my mood or energy afterward?

_____
_____
_____
_____

Day 2

- Did my mind wander, or was I able to focus?
- What quality did the light or image symbolize for me?

Day 3

- What parts of my body or heart felt most touched by the visualization?
- Did any resistance or discomfort arise?

Day 4

- Who or what did I include in the outward expansion of light?
- How did it feel to extend peace beyond myself?

Day 5

- Has anything shifted in how I see myself or others this week?
- Is there a visual image that keeps returning to me?

Day 6

- If I could embody the energy of this visualization, how would I move through my day?
- What qualities do I want to carry forward?

Day 7

- What have I learned about the creative power of my own mind?
- How might I use visualization in daily life beyond meditation?

32

BREATH COUNTING (INSPIRED BY ZEN BUDDHISM)

Count from one to ten on the breath. When you lose count, return to one. This is the Way.

— KATSUKI SEKIDA

In Zen Buddhism, *susokukan* (breath counting) is used to calm the mind and train focused awareness. The breath becomes a gate through which clarity and presence arise. This humble method can anchor even the most restless spirit.

Breath counting is traditionally taught in Rinzai and Soto Zen as an entry-level practice. It involves counting each inhalation and exhalation, usually up to ten, and gently starting over when the mind wanders. The goal is not perfection, but presence — training the attention to return, again and again.

This practice parallels other breath-based meditations across various traditions, including anapanasati in Theravāda Buddhism, pranayama in Yoga, and breath awareness in Sufism and Christian contemplative prayer. Its strength lies in its simplicity: breath, awareness, and proper alignment.

Weekly Practice: Breath Counting

Each day this week, practice breath counting (*susokukan*).

INSTRUCTIONS:

1. Sit upright in a quiet space with your spine tall and hands resting.
2. Inhale gently and mentally count "one."
3. Exhale and count "two." Continue to "ten," then return to "one."
4. If your mind wanders or you lose count, gently return to "one."
5. Practice for 5–10 minutes, gradually increasing time through the week.

Returning to your breath is returning to yourself. In the rhythm of inhale and exhale, you may discover a still center through quiet repetition. Breath by breath, count by count, the mind softens and the spirit steadies.

Reflection Journal

D_{AY} 1

- Was it easy or difficult to stay with the breath count?
- What distracted you most?

_____
_____
_____
_____

Day 2

- How did it feel to gently begin again after losing count?
- Did any sensations or emotions arise?

Day 3

- What patterns are you noticing in your breath or attention?
- Do you judge yourself when distracted?

Day 4

- Did the breath feel different today — slower, deeper, or shallower?
- Was there any shift in your mental state after practice?

Day 5

- How has this simple practice affected your mood or focus during the day?
- What's been the most surprising part?

Day 6

- Did your awareness feel more stable today?
- How has your relationship with your breath changed?

Day 7

- What have you learned about your mind through this practice?
- How might this breath counting carry into moments of daily stress or challenge?
- What will you carry forward from this week into your larger spiritual journey?

33

NAMING THE INNER CRITIC (INSPIRED BY JUNGIAN PSYCHOLOGY)

Until you make the unconscious conscious, it will direct your life and you will call it fate.
Carl Jung

Most of us carry an internal voice that judges, doubts, or undermines us, often inherited from past experiences or cultural conditioning. In Jungian psychology, this voice is part of the "shadow," the unconscious parts of ourselves that need integration, not repression. By naming and dialoging with your inner critic, you begin a path of healing and inner freedom.

Carl Jung's concept of the "shadow" refers to the hidden aspects of the self, encompassing not only negative traits but also creativity, strength, and potential that have been suppressed. Within the shadow lives the inner critic, a voice that often mimics past authority figures, cultural shame, or childhood wounds. Jung believed that healing requires recognizing these parts, naming them, and forming a conscious relationship. Naming the critic helps separate your true self from this voice, creating space for compassion and self-acceptance.

Weekly Practice: Naming the Inner Critic

This week, bring the inner critic into the light.

INSTRUCTIONS:

1. At the end of each day, reflect on any moment of self-judgment or harsh inner talk.
2. Write it down exactly as it occurred.
3. Ask: Who does this voice sound like? Is it protecting you, or limiting you?
4. Give it a name or image (e.g., "The Judge," "The Worrier," "The Phantom Teacher").
5. Begin a compassionate inner dialogue. What would your wise self say in response?

The inner critic loses its power when seen clearly. By naming and understanding it, you reclaim your inner authority and begin to relate to yourself with the same kindness you offer others. This is not self-indulgence; it is soul work.

Reflection Journal

DAY 1

- When did the inner critic show up today?
- What words did it use? How did it make you feel?

_____
_____
_____
_____

Day 2

- Can you identify where this voice originated (a person, a belief, an event)?
- What does this critic think it's protecting you from?

Day 3

- Give your inner critic a name or image.
- If you drew it, what would it look like?

Day 4

- Write a short letter to your inner critic. What do you want it to know?
- What would your most compassionate self say to you today?

Day 5

- Did the critic appear in a moment when you were trying something new or vulnerable?
- How might you shift from criticism to curiosity?

Day 6

- What would life look like if this voice softened?
- Are there any inner allies that speak more gently? Describe them.

Day 7

- How has this week changed your relationship with your inner voice?
- What do you now understand about your inner critic that you didn't before?
- How will you continue to respond when this voice arises in the future?

34
INTENTION SETTING (INSPIRED BY SANKALPA, YOGA NIDRA)

You are your deepest driving desire.

— CHANDOGYA UPANISHAD *3.14.1*

A *sankalpa* is a sacred vow aligned with your soul's true nature. In yogic philosophy, especially during the deeply relaxed state of *Yoga Nidra* (yogic sleep), the mind becomes fertile ground for planting these intentions. When practiced regularly, a *sankalpa* becomes a quiet inner compass, drawing your life into alignment with your highest values and aspirations.

In Sanskrit, *sankalpa* (resolve or will), but within yoga traditions, it refers to a deep intention or affirmation that expresses one's highest truth. Unlike surface-level goals, a *sankalpa* is stated in the present tense and affirms an already-present quality (e.g., "I am grounded," not "I will try to be grounded").

Yoga Nidra is a state of conscious deep relaxation where the body sleeps, but the mind remains awake. In this receptive state, the subconscious is especially open to suggestion. A *sankalpa* repeated here can take root far beneath habitual thoughts, reshaping inner patterns over time.

Weekly Practice: Intention Setting

This week, choose a *sankalpa* and return to it daily, especially during times of rest or before sleep.

INSTRUCTIONS:

1. Reflect on a quality or truth your soul longs to embody (e.g., peace, strength, healing, clarity).
2. Create a brief, positive statement in the present tense (e.g., "I am enough," "I choose trust," "I live from love.")
3. Each night before falling asleep, repeat your *sankalpa* mentally 3–5 times.
4. Optionally, use it during meditation, deep breathing, or after Yoga Nidra.

A *sankalpa* is not about effort; it is about alignment. When you return to your chosen intention each day, you strengthen the roots of your true self. In stillness and repetition, your inner vow begins to shape your outer life.

Reflection Journal

Day 1

- What quality does your soul long to embody right now?
- Write your *sankalpa*. How does it feel when you say it?

_____
_____
_____
_____

Day 2

- Did your *sankalpa* arise naturally today? If not, when might you have needed it?
- What emotions or resistance did you notice?

Day 3

- Where in your body do you feel the effects of this intention?
- Did it influence your choices or mindset today?

Day 4

- What would change in your life if this *sankalpa* fully manifested?
- Are you beginning to believe it more deeply?

Day 5

- Was there a moment today that tested your *sankalpa*?
- How did you respond, and what did you learn?

Day 6

- Have you noticed subtle shifts in your thoughts, energy, or actions this week?
- What old belief is your *sankalpa* beginning to replace?

Day 7

- How has this intention shaped your week?
- Will you continue with the same *sankalpa* or choose a new one going forward?

35
MANTRA MEDITATION (INSPIRED BY HINDUISM/ VEDANTA)

Om is the bow, the soul is the arrow, and Brahman is the target.

— MUNDAKA UPANISHAD 2.2.4

A mantra is more than just a word; it is a vibration, an intention, and a spiritual focus all in one. Rooted in Hinduism and used across Buddhist, Jain, and Sikh traditions, mantras are sacred syllables or phrases repeated to calm the mind and invoke higher consciousness. Chanting a mantra can realign your energy, anchor your awareness, and open your heart to the divine.

The Sanskrit word mantra comes from the roots *man* (mind) and *tra* (instrument or tool), thus translating to "a tool of thought." In Hindu traditions, mantras such as *Om, So Hum,* or *Om Shanti* are repeated during meditation to elevate consciousness or focus devotional energy. Some mantras invoke specific deities, while others point to universal truths. The mantra *Om* is considered the primordial sound — the vibration of creation itself. Reciting mantras is a central part of *japa* yoga (the yoga of repetition), often done with mala beads to count each recitation.

Weekly Practice: Mantra Meditation

This week, choose a mantra and work with it daily to focus your mind and steady your energy.

INSTRUCTIONS:

1. Choose a mantra that resonates with you (*Om, So Hum, Om Shanti*, or a personal sacred word).
2. Sit comfortably with eyes closed.
3. Begin repeating the mantra aloud or silently for 5–15 minutes.
4. Let the rhythm and sound guide your breath and awareness.
5. If distracted, gently return to the mantra without judgment.

Repeating a mantra can center the mind, soften the heart, and attune your spirit to something greater. In its repetition, you may discover the stillness beneath the noise and the divine presence within.

Reflection Journal

DAY 1

- Which mantra did you choose, and why?
- How did it feel to say or hear it repeatedly?

_____
_____
_____

Day 2

- What distracted you during today's practice?
- Were you able to return to your mantra with compassion?

Day 3

- How does your body feel during and after chanting?
- Are you noticing changes in your breath, posture, or energy?

Day 4

- Does your mantra carry any emotional weight or memory?
- What does it seem to awaken in you?

Day 5

- What resistance (if any) are you encountering in this practice?
- How might you move through it gently?

Day 6

- Have you begun to carry your mantra into your day (e.g., during stress)?
- How has that affected your mindset or reactions?

Day 7

- What has your mantra practice revealed about your inner landscape?
- Do you feel closer to your intention, stillness, or source?

36
KINTSUGI (INSPIRED BY JAPANESE PHILOSOPHY)

The true life of the bowl began the moment it was dropped.

— CHRISTY BARTLETT

Kintsugi is a Japanese art form that involves repairing broken pottery with lacquer mixed with powdered gold. Instead of hiding the cracks, the breakage is highlighted, celebrated as part of the object's story. It's a powerful metaphor for the human experience: our scars are not shameful; they are evidence of survival and transformation. What if your wounds weren't flaws, but golden seams of wisdom?

Kintsugi (golden joinery) and dates to the 15th century. It is rooted in the Japanese philosophy of *wabi-sabi*, which embraces imperfection, impermanence, and the natural wear of time. *Kintsugi* artists believe that an object is more beautiful for having been broken, because its history becomes part of its unique design.

In the context of Zen Buddhist influence, this practice becomes more than a mere aesthetic; it becomes a spiritual metaphor for resilience. Just as the bowl becomes more precious after repair, so can we reclaim our brokenness with grace.

Weekly Practice: *Kintsugi*

This week, use the wisdom of *kintsugi* to explore how your past wounds have shaped your beauty and strength.

INSTRUCTIONS:

1. Reflect on a time in your life when you felt "broken" — physically, emotionally, spiritually, or relationally.
2. Write a compassionate letter to that past version of yourself. Honor the growth that has come from the pain.
3. Optional: If you have a broken object (mug, plate, figurine), repair it with glue and decorate the seams with gold paint or pen. Let it symbolize your healing.

Kintsugi teaches that our cracks are not failures. They are the places where light enters. When we choose to embrace our scars as part of our sacred wholeness, we discover a beauty that is more honest, humble, and strong.

Reflection Journal

Day 1

- What does "brokenness" mean to you personally?
- Are there parts of your story you still try to hide or ignore?

_____
_____
_____
_____
_____

Day 2

- Choose one wound or break you carry.
- How has it shaped your outlook, relationships, or self-concept?

Day 3

- What "gold" has emerged from that experience (e.g., compassion, resilience)?
- Would you trade it if it meant never being broken?

Day 4

- How do you respond when others share their brokenness with you?
- Can you extend that same grace to yourself?

Day 5

- If your scars could speak, what would they want to be honored for?
- What do they ask you to remember?

Day 6

- Is there an object in your life that symbolizes healing or survival?
- What story does it carry?

Day 7

- How might you begin to live as if your imperfections are sacred?
- What might change in your life if you embraced your whole self, cracks and all?

37
PLANTING AS PRAYER (INSPIRED BY INDIGENOUS, AGRARIAN, AND EARTH-BASED TRADITIONS)

The seed is a promise of the future.

— *DINÉ*

To place a seed in the earth is to join in the mystery of life. It is a gesture of surrender and hope, a quiet invocation for growth. Across Indigenous and agrarian societies, planting is not merely an agricultural practice; it is a ceremonial one. A seed carries more than genetic code; it carries prayer, memory, and possibility.

In many cultures, the act of planting is sacred because it mirrors the human journey. We enter dark places. We wait. We root down before we rise. The soil becomes an altar. The hands become instruments of blessing. To plant with intention is to reconnect with the land, the ancestors who tilled it, and the unseen life waiting to emerge. Even in small acts (one seed, one pot, one handful of earth) we rejoin the ancient rhythm of creation.

In the Iroquois (*Haudenosaunee*) tradition, the "Three Sisters" (corn, beans, and squash) are more than crops; they are sacred kin. Planted together in harmony, they nourish the soil and each other,

teaching the values of cooperation, balance, and interdependence.*
Across Indigenous nations, planting is often preceded by song, prayer, or an offering (such as tobacco, water, or cornmeal) to honor the land and ask permission before disturbing it. These ceremonies acknowledge that we are not owners of the earth, but participants in a living system.

Similar rituals span the globe: African communities pour libations into the soil before planting; Celtic traditions involve planting trees on sacred days; in Japanese Shinto, farmers once invited the *kami* (nature spirits) to bless the fields each spring.† All speak to a shared truth: that planting is more than survival; it is spiritual alignment with the cycles of life

Weekly Practice: Planting as Prayer

Instructions:

1. Choose a seed or small plant that is easy to grow (herbs, beans, wildflowers, or a small tree).
2. Prepare the soil slowly and mindfully. Touch it with reverence. Smell the earth. Speak gratitude aloud or silently.
3. Place the seed into the ground or a pot, and as you do, say a prayer, blessing, or quiet intention. Example: *"May what is planted in love grow in beauty and balance."*
4. Water the seed gently. Offer your breath, your hope, or a song.
5. Return each day to witness its growth or simply to sit in stillness with it. Let this be a practice in patience and presence.

---

* Robin Wall Kimmerer, *Braiding Sweetgrass: Indigenous Wisdom, Scientific Knowledge, and the Teachings of Plants*(Minneapolis: Milkweed Editions, 2013), 128–135.
† Martín Prechtel, *The Unlikely Peace at Cuchumaquic: The Parallel Lives of People as Plants* (Berkeley, CA: North Atlantic Books, 2012), 62–69.

Planting reminds us that transformation is slow, sacred, and often hidden. The seed does not rush. It knows how to rest in darkness before rising in light. To plant is to trust. To tend is to believe in what you cannot yet see. In honoring the seed, you honor your becoming, your rootedness, your quiet power, your capacity to bloom. You do not need to know how everything will unfold. You need only to plant, tend, and believe.

Reflection Journal

Day 1

- What did this small act stir in your spirit?
- What parallels do you see between planting and beginning something new in your life?
- What hopes or emotions did you offer into the soil?

_____
_____
_____
_____
_____
_____
_____
_____
_____

Day 2

- In what area of your life are you being called to show up with steady care?

- What small action today felt like "watering" your inner growth?

_____
_____
_____
_____
_____
_____
_____
_____

Day 3

- How do you relate to the idea of unseen growth happening in the dark?
- What parts of your life are in the "soil" phase — developing invisibly but deeply?

_____
_____
_____
_____
_____
_____
_____
_____

Day 4

- What is it teaching you about patience, process, or beauty?
- How does this interaction shift your view of time or success?

_____
_____
_____
_____
_____
_____
_____
_____

Day 5

- Which season of the cycle are you currently in?
- How can you honor your current pace without rushing?

_____
_____
_____
_____
_____
_____
_____
_____

Day 6

- What are you most grateful for in the natural world?
- How do you see yourself in relationship with the Earth, not above it?

_____
_____
_____
_____
_____
_____
_____
_____

Day 7

- What spiritual insights or emotional shifts have blossomed?
- What is one intention you want to carry forward from this practice?

_____
_____
_____
_____
_____
_____
_____
_____

38

SOUND BATHING (INSPIRED BY TIBETAN BOWLS AND GLOBAL TRADITIONS)

Sound will be the medicine of the future.

— EDGAR CAYCE

Across cultures, sound has long been used as a gateway to healing, meditation, and altered states of consciousness. In Tibetan and Himalayan traditions, sound bathing involves immersing the body and mind in harmonic vibrations produced by singing bowls, gongs, or chimes. These frequencies help relax the nervous system and guide the brain into a meditative state. Whether you use traditional instruments or recorded tones, this practice invites you to receive sound as nourishment for body and soul.

Tibetan singing bowls are believed to have originated as ritual objects and meditation tools, with use dating back over a thousand years. Typically made from a blend of metals, each bowl produces rich, layered tones when struck or circled with a mallet. These sounds can induce theta and delta brainwave states, associated with deep relaxation and restoration. Similar sound healing traditions exist globally, including the use of crystal bowls in modern wellness, gongs in Southeast Asia, and drumming or rattling in Indigenous healing ceremonies.

Weekly Practice: Sound Bathing

INSTRUCTIONS:

1. Find a quiet, comfortable place to lie down or sit.
2. Play a singing bowl yourself, use chimes, or listen to a sound bath recording.
3. Let the vibrations pass through you. Focus on the sensations.
4. If thoughts arise, return your attention gently to the sound.
5. Note: This is a receptive practice. There is no need to "do" anything but listen.

When you bathe in sacred sound, you enter a space beyond words. Let the tones carry you into stillness, helping you release tension, balance your energy, and reconnect with inner harmony.

Reflection Journal

DAY 1

- What did you notice in your body as the sound began?
- Did any part of you resist relaxation?
- How did the experience affect your breath or thoughts?

_____

_____

Day 2

- What sounds or tones stood out most today?
- Where did the sound "land" in your body?
- Did any emotions rise unexpectedly?

Day 3

- What was it like to simply receive sound without trying to interpret it?
- Did you feel more present, or did your mind wander?

- How might this teach you about surrender?

Day 4

- Did today's session feel different from earlier ones?
- What thoughts, if any, seemed to "melt away" with the sound?
- How do you relate to the idea of sound as energetic cleansing?

Day 5

- Did the sounds take you to a deeper state today?
- What physical sensations or shifts in awareness did you notice?
- How would you describe the silence after the sound ended?

Day 6

- Did the experience offer insight or peace beyond language?
- What images, memories, or symbols arose (if any)?
- How is this different from other forms of meditation you've tried?

Day 7

- Looking back on the week, how has your relationship to sound or silence changed?
- What are you taking with you from this practice?
- Can you imagine returning to sound bathing regularly?

39

SACRED WEEPING (INSPIRED BY JEWISH, SUFI, AND INDIGENOUS TRADITIONS)

God counts your tears.

— *TALMUD, BERAKHOT 32B*

Tears are not a failure of strength; they are a release, a revelation, and sometimes even a form of prayer. Across spiritual traditions, sacred weeping is seen as a breakthrough, not as a breakdown. In Jewish mysticism, tears are believed to be collected by God. In Sufi poetry, weeping is a sign of the heart's longing. In many Indigenous rituals, crying is encouraged as part of cleansing and healing ceremonies. Tears can be a bridge between the visible and the invisible, a language of the soul when words fall short.

In Judaism, sacred texts like the Talmud speak of tears as prayers heard by God, especially in moments of silent anguish. The Hasidic masters also viewed weeping during prayer as a sign of divine intimacy. Sufi poets like Rumi and Hafiz wrote about the tears of lovers dissolving the veil between the self and the Divine. Among Indigenous cultures, such as the Lakota, crying ceremonies accompany sweat lodges, grief rituals, and rites of passage as a way to purify and honor deep emotional truth.

Weekly Practice: Sacred Weeping

This week, give yourself sacred permission to feel and to weep.

INSTRUCTIONS:

1. Set aside quiet time each day to reflect on something tender or unresolved.
2. Invite your emotions to rise without judgment.
3. If tears come, let them flow as an offering to healing, to Spirit, to yourself.
4. Afterward, place your hand on your heart in compassion.
5. **Note:** Sacred weeping is never forced. Some days may be dry. Honor the silence as much as the tears.

Tears carry what the soul cannot say. They cleanse, soften, and reconnect us to the deepest truths. To weep is to let Spirit move through you in liquid form (prayer, healing, and honesty in one sacred act).

Reflective Journal

DAY 1

- What emotions surfaced when you created space for reflection today?
- Did you resist or welcome them?
- If you didn't cry, did your body feel the impulse?

_____
_____
_____

Day 2

- How did you speak to yourself around your emotions today?
- Did tears come, and if so, what triggered them?
- How can you honor what you feel without labeling it?

Day 3

- Where did you feel emotion in your body today?
- Did the act of weeping (or trying to) change your breath or heartbeat?

- What memories, if any, accompanied the emotion?

_____
_____
_____
_____
_____
_____
_____
_____
_____
_____

Day 4

- Could you see your tears (or your effort to feel) as a gift rather than a burden?
- What are your tears trying to release?
- To whom (or what) might you be offering them?

_____
_____
_____
_____
_____
_____
_____
_____
_____

Day 5

- What is something you grieve but rarely speak of?
- Did making space for that pain bring relief, insight, or discomfort?
- How can grief be part of your spiritual life?

Day 6

- How did your relationship to your emotions shift over the week?
- What did your tears (or lack of them) teach you today?
- What is something tender you want to protect or nurture?

Day 7

- Reflect on the week. What surprised you?
- What is one truth that emerged through the practice?
- How can you continue to make space for sacred weeping in your life?

40

SACRED OFFERING (INSPIRED BY THE SHINTO TRADITION OF OSAISEN)

Offer with sincerity, and the divine hears not your words, but your heart.

— SHINTO MAXIM

Across cultures and spiritual paths, the act of offering (giving something intentionally and with reverence) has been a means of expressing gratitude, humility, and connection. In Shinto, this practice is known as *osaisen*, a form of symbolic offering to the *kami*, the divine spirits that dwell in all things. Offerings are not made to earn favor, but to return a portion of what we have received with sincerity and care. Whether it is a coin, a flower, a word of thanks, or a thoughtful gesture, the offering becomes sacred when it flows from a heart filled with awareness.

Traditionally, in Shinto, people approach a shrine, toss a coin into the offering box, bow twice, clap twice, and silently share a prayer before bowing again. This practice centers on respect, sincerity (*magokoro*), and a harmonious relationship with the natural and spiritual world.*

But you don't need to be at a shrine (or follow a specific tradition) to experience the spiritual impact of offering. You might offer a moment of silence in nature, a gesture of kindness to another person, or a symbolic object placed on an altar or windowsill. What matters most is your intention: to give without expectation, to honor life itself, and to remember that gratitude is a sacred form of connection.[†]

Weekly Practice: *Osaisen*

This week, we open ourselves to the practice of offering, not as an obligation, but as an invitation to participate in the ongoing cycle of giving and receiving that sustains the world.

INSTRUCTION:

1. Each day this week, choose one simple offering—an object, gesture, word, or moment.
2. Place it or perform it with mindfulness and gratitude.
3. Say inwardly: *"This is given with sincerity and thanks."*
4. Let the practice be enough, offering without needing anything in return.

The world is full of unseen exchanges; sunlight feeding the earth, rivers carrying water, people sharing breath. When we offer from the heart, we become participants in this sacred exchange. May your offerings this week, no matter how small, remind you that you are part of something vast, beautiful, and alive.

---

* Ian Reader and George J. Tanabe Jr., *Practically Religious: Worldly Benefits and the Common Religion of Japan* (Honolulu: University of Hawai'i Press, 1998), 55–56.
† Motohisa Yamakage, *The Essence of Shinto: Japan's Spiritual Heart*, trans. Mineko A. McElhiney (Tokyo: Kodansha International, 2006), 109–112.

Reflection Journal

<u>Day 1</u>

- What does it mean to offer something with no strings attached?
- How do you feel when you give without expecting acknowledgment or reward?
- What is one thing you could offer today from a place of gratitude?

_____
_____
_____
_____
_____
_____
_____
_____
_____
_____

<u>Day 2</u>

- What has life gifted you recently—tangible or intangible?
- How can you respond to that gift with a meaningful act or offering?
- What small gesture today could carry deep sincerity?

_____
_____
_____

Day 3

- When do you feel most connected to the flow of giving and receiving?
- How might nature or your environment invite you into sacred reciprocity?
- What would it look like to offer presence as a gift?

Day 4

- Who or what has shaped you in quiet, lasting ways?
- What might an offering of remembrance or honor look like for them?
- How does expressing gratitude through action feel in your body?

_____
_____
_____
_____
_____
_____
_____
_____
_____
_____
_____
_____

Day 5

- What barriers (mental or emotional) keep you from offering freely?
- What would it mean to release those just for today?
- Can generosity become a form of personal healing?

_____
_____

Day 6

- What every day routines could be transformed into rituals of offering?
- How does your intention shape the energy of what you give?
- What beauty can you offer to the world today?

Day 7

- Reflect on the week. How did the act of offering affect your inner world?
- What did you learn about your relationship with gratitude and surrender?
- How might this practice continue to ripple through your life?

41

MINDFUL EATING (INSPIRED BY BUDDHIST AND AYURVEDIC TRADITIONS)

When eating, just eat.

— ZEN TEACHING

In both Buddhism and Ayurveda, eating is not just nourishment. Eating is a sacred act of presence. Food is viewed not as fuel alone but as a gift: from the earth, from those who grew and prepared it, and from the life force (*prana*) within it. To eat mindfully is to slow down and awaken to the miracle of sustenance, recognizing that how we eat is just as important as what we eat. Mindful eating invites us to be present, to taste, feel, and honor the journey of our food. In doing so, we return to a core truth shared across many traditions. That gratitude and attention turns even a simple meal into a sacred ritual.

In Buddhism, the practice of mindful eating is often taught during retreats and monastic life. Practitioners are guided to chew slowly, eat in silence, and bring full awareness to each bite. This allows them to perceive the interconnectedness of all things, from the soil to the rain to the cook's hands.*

Ayurveda, the ancient healing science of India, similarly teaches that food should be eaten in a peaceful environment, with full presence, and without distraction. Eating in silence is said to support digestion, balance energy, and deepen one's connection to the wisdom of the body.†

Weekly Practice: Mindful Eating

Together, these traditions remind us that food is more than just a means of consumption; it is a form of communion.

INSTRUCTIONS:

1. Once each day this week, eat one meal or snack in total silence.
2. Set your phone aside. Turn off music and screens. Be fully present.
3. Before eating, pause. Take a few deep breaths. Offer thanks in your own way.
4. Eat slowly. Chew fully. Notice colors, textures, and sensations.
5. When thoughts arise, gently return attention to your food.

Mindful eating is an invitation to presence and reverence. When we slow down and honor the sacred process of nourishment, we not only care for our bodies, we train our hearts in gratitude, simplicity, and joy. May each meal this week become a quiet doorway into deeper awareness.

---

* Thich Nhat Hanh, *How to Eat* (Berkeley, CA: Parallax Press, 2014), 12–17.
† Vasant Lad, *The Complete Book of Ayurvedic Home Remedies* (New York: Harmony Books, 1999), 63–66.

Reflection Journal

Day 1

- How do you usually experience meals—rushed, distracted, or mindful?
- What emotions or habits tend to show up when you eat?
- What would it mean to turn eating into a spiritual practice?

_____
_____
_____
_____
_____
_____
_____
_____
_____

Day 2

- As you eat in silence today, what did you notice that surprised you?
- How did the pace of your eating shift?
- What feelings or memories came up while eating mindfully?

_____
_____
_____

Day 3

- What is one thing you're grateful for about the meal you ate today?
- Who or what helped bring that food to your plate?
- How does gratitude affect your sense of fullness or satisfaction?

Day 4

- Was it difficult to eat without distractions? Why or why not?
- What did your body feel like before, during, and after the meal?
- How might silence be a source of nourishment?

Day 5

- What kinds of food feel most nourishing to you—physically, emotionally, or spiritually?
- How do you want to approach your next meal with intention?
- What does your body need to feel supported and cared for?

Day 6

- Reflect on how your relationship with food has changed over time.
- How have culture, faith, or family influenced your eating habits?
- What would it look like to bring more awareness and compassion to your meals?

Day 7

- Looking back on this week, what did mindful eating teach you?
- How did silence and presence shape your experience of food and self?
- How might you carry this practice forward in everyday life?

42

FIRE GAZING (INSPIRED BY ZOROASTRIAN AND INDIGENOUS SHAMANIC TRADITIONS)

Where there is fire, there is the witness of the sacred.

— ZOROASTRIAN PRINCIPLE

For millennia, fire has symbolized light, wisdom, transformation, and connection to the sacred. In Zoroastrianism, fire is a visible symbol of divine presence—eternal, luminous, and life-giving.* In many Indigenous and shamanic traditions, fire is honored as a teacher and portal, connecting the seen and unseen, the earthly and the ancestral. In both, fire is not merely a tool; it is a living force that listens, reveals, and purifies.

Zoroastrian temples maintain ever-burning sacred fires, which are not worshipped but revered as symbols of *asha* (truth, divine order, and righteousness). Practitioners meditate in its presence, seeking clarity and connection to the sacred.† Similarly, fire is central in many shamanic practices. It is treated as an elder, a keeper of

---

* Mary Boyce, *Zoroastrians: Their Religious Beliefs and Practices*, 2nd ed. (London: Routledge, 2001), 54–56.
† Jenny Rose, *Zoroastrianism: An Introduction* (London: I.B. Tauris, 2011), 77–79.

stories, and a messenger between worlds. To sit with fire is to listen and learn, not with the mind, but with the heart. One need not belong to any one tradition to benefit from this practice; reverently observing fire in silence can ground, calm, and awaken anyone willing to be still.*

Weekly Practice: Fire Gazing

To sit with fire (whether a blazing fire or a single candle) is to return to ancient ways of prayer and presence. Fire gazing invites us into stillness, offering warmth to the body and illumination to the spirit.

INSTRUCTIONS:

1. Sit in a quiet space with a fire, fireplace, or candle.
2. Dim other lights. Allow the flame to be your only illumination.
3. Watch its movement. Notice how it dances, flickers, pulses.
4. Listen not with ears, but with presence. Let thoughts rise and fall like sparks.
5. Stay for at least 10 minutes. No need to "do," just be.

In a world of constant light and noise, fire gazing invites us back to the ancient intimacy of being still before something primal and sacred. Let the flame mirror your inner fire. Let it speak in silence. Let it remind you that transformation begins in stillness, not struggle.

---

* Alberto Villoldo, *Shaman, Healer, Sage: How to Heal Yourself and Others with the Energy Medicine of the Americas*(New York: Harmony Books, 2000), 98–103.

Reflection Journal

Day 1

- When was the last time you simply sat and watched a flame?
- What does fire symbolize to you—emotionally, spiritually, or energetically?
- How do you feel when you give yourself permission to be still?

Day 2

- As you gazed at the fire or candle today, what thoughts or sensations surfaced?
- Did the flame's movement mirror anything in your current emotional state?
- What does "listening with presence" mean to you?

Day 3

- What in your life feels ready to be transformed or released?
- If fire could speak to you today, what might it say?
- How might sitting with fire shift your perspective or energy?

Day 4

- How does fire connect you to your ancestry, lineage, or cultural memory?
- What role has ritual or ceremony played in your spiritual development?
- What sacred stories live within you that need tending or rekindling?

_____
_____
_____
_____
_____
_____
_____
_____
_____
_____

Day 5

- In what ways has your inner fire been dimmed—and how might it be reignited?
- What fuels your passion and spiritual vitality?
- What distracts you from sitting with your own inner flame?

_____
_____
_____
_____
_____

Day 6

- As you sat with fire today, how did your breath respond?
- What does the dance of flame teach you about impermanence and beauty?
- What if silence itself is a form of prayer?

Day 7

- Reflect on your experience of fire gazing this week. What shifted?
- How can you honor fire—not only as an element, but as a spiritual ally?
- What do you now know, feel, or see more clearly?

43

LISTENING TO THE LAND (INSPIRED BY THE CHEROKEE TRADITION)

The land remembers everything. Listen long enough, and it will teach you who you are.

— CHEROKEE TEACHING

For the Cherokee people, as with many Indigenous nations, the earth is a relative. The land is living, breathing, and communicating. In Cherokee cosmology, all of nature (plants, stones, winds, animals) is considered part of the sacred web of life known as *unolevwiya*: the world in right relationship.[*] Listening to the land is a form of prayer, a way to remember who we are and where we come from.

Cherokee spiritual practice emphasizes reciprocity with nature, giving thanks, walking gently, and listening deeply. The land is not viewed as something to be owned or conquered, but as a conscious being deserving of respect. Elders teach that every plant and tree

---

[*] J.T. Garrett and Michael Garrett, *The Cherokee Full Circle: A Practical Guide to Ceremonies and Traditions* (Rochester, VT: Bear & Company, 2002), 23–26.

have its song, and every part of the natural world holds memory.* This teaching resonates across Indigenous traditions, where silence and listening are regarded as powerful spiritual tools. Spending time in nature, in intentional stillness, is a way to restore balance—what the Cherokee call *udalvltanv* (harmony). † You don't need to be Cherokee to practice this form of reverence. Simply going outside and listening with humility and gratitude can be a gateway to healing and reconnection.

Weekly Practice: Listening to the Land

This week, you are invited to step outside, touch the ground, and listen. Not to speak or seek answers but to practice the ancient art of respect, silence, and presence with the more-than-human world.

Instructions:

1. Each day, spend at least 10 minutes in nature—barefoot if possible.
2. Sit or stand quietly with a tree, stream, hill, or patch of earth.
3. Say inwardly: *"I am here to listen. I honor your spirit."*
4. Stay in silence. Let the sounds, textures, and sensations guide you.
5. Leave a small offering if you wish—like water, cornmeal, or a breath of thanks.

When we stop to listen, the land speaks not in words, but in knowing. This week, let your practice be simple: slow down, make contact, and listen with your whole being. In that silence, you may hear the voice of creation.

---

* Robin Wall Kimmerer, *Braiding Sweetgrass: Indigenous Wisdom, Scientific Knowledge, and the Teachings of Plants*(Minneapolis: Milkweed Editions, 2013), 42–49.
† J.T. Garrett, *Medicine of the Cherokee: The Way of Right Relationship* (Rochester, VT: Bear & Company, 1996), 115–118.

Reflection Journal

Day 1

- What does the land mean to you—emotionally, spiritually, or ancestrally?
- How often do you pause to listen, rather than speak or think?
- What place in nature has always felt like a teacher to you?

Day 2

- As you sat with the land today, what sensations arose in your body?
- What did you see, hear, or feel that you might have missed before
- How does your energy shift when you're fully present outdoors?

Day 3

- What would it mean to consider nature as alive, aware, and communicative?
- What questions might you carry into your next listening session?
- What parts of you feel more grounded or open after time on the earth?

. . .

Day 4

- What stories or memories might the land around you carry?
- How can you begin to build a more reciprocal relationship with your environment?
- What does humility feel like when you're in the presence of nature?

_____
_____
_____
_____
_____
_____
_____
_____
_____
_____
_____

Day 5

- What are you noticing about your breath, pace, or attention during this practice?
- What happens when you let go of needing answers and simply receive?
- What wisdom might the natural world be offering you today?

Day 6

- Reflect on the voice of the land—what does "listening" mean in this context?
- How do stillness and respect deepen your sense of connection?
- What emotional or spiritual messages surfaced during your time outdoors?

Day 7

- How has this week changed your relationship with the land or your surroundings?
- What do you want to remember from this experience moving forward?
- What practice will help you keep listening even in daily, busy life?

44

THE QUIET HOUR (INSPIRED BY AMISH CONTEMPLATIVE LIVING)

Let thy quietness shine. It may be louder than words.

— AMISH PROVERB

In a world of noise and speed, the Amish offer a countertestimony: a life grounded in simplicity, silence, and shared purpose. Although often associated with outward practices such as plain dress and a lack of technology, the heart of Amish spirituality lies in inward stillness. This stillness is cultivated through quiet reflection, communal rhythm, and personal time with God.

The "quiet hour," observed daily or weekly in many Amish homes, is not a rigid rule but a deeply valued practice. It's a time set aside to listen, to pray, or just to be.

Gelassenheit shapes the Amish spiritual worldview, a German word meaning surrender, yielding, or letting go.[*] This surrender is not passive; it is active humility, a conscious choice to slow down, be still, and let the soul align with divine rhythm. Amish communities

---

[*] Donald B. Kraybill, *The Riddle of Amish Culture*, 2nd ed. (Baltimore: Johns Hopkins University Press, 2001), 96–101.

often encourage each member to find time daily for quiet contemplation, usually after chores or before supper, to read Scripture, reflect, or pray.*

The quiet hour may include reading sacred texts, but it can also be silent time in a chair by the window, walking in solitude, or tending a garden mindfully. The emphasis is not on performance, but on presence. Creating space for what cannot be heard amid the world's noise.

Weekly Practice: Quiet Hour

This week, you are invited to create your own quiet hour, to unplug, sit in silence, and listen for the voice within.

Instructions:

1. Set aside 30–60 minutes each day this week for a "quiet hour."
2. Turn off all electronics. Let others know you'll be offline.
3. Sit, walk, read sacred text, or simply be in silence.
4. Begin with a short phrase such as: *"I surrender this hour to peace and presence."*
5. Let whatever arises come and go without fixing, judging, or rushing.

Silence is not the absence of sound; it is the presence of depth. In the quiet hour, we return to what matters. Like the Amish, we learn that true strength is gentle, and that listening can be more transformative than speaking. This week, may you rediscover the voice that speaks in stillness.

---

* Steven M. Nolt, *A History of the Amish*, rev. ed. (Intercourse, PA: Good Books, 2003), 221–225.

Reflection Journal

Day 1

- How often do you allow yourself to sit in silence with no agenda?
- What does your inner world sound like when there's no outside noise?
- What might you gain from protecting one hour each day from distraction?

Day 2

- What arose during your quiet hour today—emotionally or spiritually?
- Was it hard or easy to sit still? Why do you think that is?
- What are you beginning to hear beneath the surface of your thoughts?

Day 3

- Reflect on your relationship with stillness. Does it feel safe? Foreign? Restful?
- What part of your life might benefit from more quiet attention?
- What truths become clearer when there is nothing to interrupt them?

Day 4

- How does the simplicity of the quiet hour contrast with the rest of your day?
- What emotions or insights did the stillness reveal today?
- What's one thing you'd like to surrender or release during this practice?

_____
_____
_____
_____
_____
_____
_____
_____
_____
_____
_____
_____

Day 5

- What does humility mean to you—not as weakness, but as spiritual strength?
- How does being unplugged for an hour affect your body and mind?
- What might God, the Divine, or your inner self be whispering to you now?

_____
_____

Day 6

- How can you bring the peace of this hour into the rest of your day?
- What small daily habits are competing with your ability to be still?
- What does a spiritually aligned life look like to you?

Day 7

- Looking back on your quiet hours this week, what changed inside you?
- How has your perception of time, silence, or surrender shifted?
- How might you preserve this sacred space in your weekly rhythm?

45

MORNING OFFERING (INSPIRED BY THE BLACKFOOT TRADITION)

Each morning is a blessing. The East is the doorway through which life returns.

— BLACKFOOT TEACHING

In the Blackfoot tradition, mornings are sacred. Each new dawn is a gift and a ceremony. At first light, many Blackfoot elders offer tobacco, words, or silent prayers to the East, where the sun rises, and life begins again. This isn't merely habit but a spiritual orientation: a daily act of harmony, humility, and alignment with the Creator and the natural world.*

The *Niitsitapi* (Blackfoot Confederacy) view the natural world as a living system of relationships. The four cardinal directions hold spiritual significance, with the East representing beginnings, light, wisdom, and renewal. Traditional Blackfoot practice involves offering tobacco, sweetgrass, or prayers to the East at sunrise, acknowledging

---

* Betty Bastien, *Blackfoot Ways of Knowing: The Worldview of the Siksikaitsitapi*, ed. Jürgen W. Kremer (Calgary: University of Calgary Press, 2004), 89–94.

the Creator and seeking guidance, balance, and strength.* While sacred plant offerings are central in many Indigenous practices, the heart of this ritual lies in presence and humility. Even without traditional items, one can honor this rhythm by standing outdoors (or by a window), facing the dawn, breathing deeply, and offering a heartfelt intention. As with many Indigenous ceremonies, the power lies not in formality but in sincerity.†

Weekly Practice: Offering to the East

This week, you are invited to rise with the sun (or as early as possible) and greet the day not with urgency, but with reverence. Facing the East, offer your presence, breath, or a word of thanks. Begin the day in sacred relationship.

INSTRUCTIONS:

1. Rise early and go outside (or near a window) as close to sunrise as possible.
2. Face East. Stand or sit with intention.
3. Offer a word, breath, gesture, or prayer of thanks for the new day.
4. If you wish, say: "*I welcome this day with humility, clarity, and gratitude.*"
5. Stay for a few minutes in silence or speak your hopes aloud.

To greet the sun is to welcome life. This simple act can reorient our whole day. Let this week be a return to rhythm, to remembering

---

* Leroy Little Bear, "Native Science and Western Science: Possibilities for a Powerful Collaboration," *WindSpeaker*, vol. 18, no. 6 (2000): 13–15.
† Robin R. R. Gray and Chadwick Allen, "Decolonizing the Sacred: Indigenous Spirituality in Practice," in *Decolonizing Methodologies* (London: Zed Books, 2020), 121–128.

that each dawn offers the chance to begin again, in gratitude and reverence for all that lives.

Reflection Journal

Day 1

- What is your usual mindset upon waking?
- How did it feel to begin the day with a moment of sacred offering?
- What does the East—new beginnings, clarity—symbolize in your life right now?

_____
_____
_____
_____
_____
_____
_____
_____
_____
_____
_____
_____
_____

Day 2

- What emotions or intentions did you offer this morning?
- How does facing the rising sun affect your mood, energy, or awareness?

- What would it look like to treat each morning as a sacred threshold?

Day 3

- What does it mean to you to "walk in right relationship" with life?
- How does slowing down in the morning change your sense of time?
- What are you beginning, ending, or transforming in this season?

Day 4

- What messages (visual, emotional, intuitive) came during your morning offering?
- How might honoring the four directions shape your spiritual awareness?
- What does your inner compass point toward today?

Day 5

- How does your environment change in the early hours—sights, sounds, smells?
- What might it mean to be in rhythm with the land where you live?
- What guidance would you ask of the Creator, Spirit, or the ancestors?

_____
_____
_____
_____
_____
_____
_____
_____
_____
_____
_____
_____
_____

Day 6

- Reflect on how your mornings have shifted throughout this week.
- What felt natural? What felt unfamiliar?
- What would you like to carry into your morning rhythm beyond this week?

Day 7

- How has the practice of morning offering changed your sense of purpose?
- What does a spiritually grounded morning look like for you?
- How might you create a personal ritual that honors both tradition and your unique path?

46

GAZING AT THE STARS (INSPIRED BY INDIGENOUS, TAOIST, AND STOIC TRADITIONS)

Lift up your eyes to the heavens. From their silence, wisdom flows.

— TAOIST TEACHING

To look up at the stars is to remember how vast the universe is and how connected we are within it. Long before telescopes or science textbooks, people from every culture turned to the night sky for wisdom, wonder, and orientation. Indigenous elders speak of the stars as ancestors watching over us. Taoist sages describe them as expressions of the Dao's infinite rhythm. Stoic philosophers saw them as reminders of divine order, urging us to rise above the distractions of daily life.*

Among Indigenous traditions, the stars are often viewed not only as celestial bodies but as spiritual beings, guides, relatives, or storyholders. The Lakota refer to themselves as the "Star Nation," and

---

* Marcus Aurelius, *Meditations*, trans. Gregory Hays (New York: Modern Library, 2002), Book 5.

many tribes believe that the stars hold the memories of their origin and destiny.*

In Taoist cosmology, stargazing was a way of aligning oneself with the Dao, or cosmic way. The motion of stars reflected the natural balance that humans were called to embody, humble, harmonious, and flowing with the rhythm of life.†

The Stoics, such as Marcus Aurelius, encouraged contemplation of the night sky to put human concerns into perspective. When you gaze at the stars, he wrote, you remember that your soul is of the same stuff as the heavens, rational, enduring, and ordered.‡

Weekly Practice: Stargazing

This week, you are invited to return to the ancient practice of skywatching for transformation. No words, no agenda. Just silence, stillness, and awe beneath the stars.

INSTRUCTIONS:

1. Choose a clear night and step outside.
2. Sit or stand in silence. Look up at the stars.
3. Let your breath slow. Say inwardly: *"I belong to the vastness."*
4. Notice how the stars move, shimmer, or pulse.
5. Stay for at least 10 minutes. No phones, no speaking. Just presence.

To gaze at the stars is to let the sacred reorient you. This week, let the sky be your sanctuary. Let your worries shrink beneath its bril-

---

* Vine Deloria Jr., *God Is Red: A Native View of Religion*, 30th Anniversary ed. (Golden, CO: Fulcrum Publishing, 2003), 84–87.
† Eva Wong, *Taoism: An Essential Guide* (Boston: Shambhala, 2011), 145–148.
‡ Pierre Hadot, *The Inner Citadel: The Meditations of Marcus Aurelius*, trans. Michael Chase (Cambridge, MA: Harvard University Press, 1998), 131–135.

liance. Let the mystery remind you: you are not lost. You are part of something ancient, expansive, and beautiful beyond words.

Reflection Journal

Day 1

- When was the last time you truly looked at the stars?
- What emotions or thoughts surfaced as you gazed tonight?
- What does "vastness" mean to you—not intellectually, but spiritually?

Day 2

- Did the silence of the sky feel comforting, intimidating, or something else?
- What shifted in your body or mind as you gazed longer?
- How does your view of daily problems change when compared to the cosmos?

Day 3

- If the stars could speak, what might they say to you tonight?
- What stories or memories do the stars hold for you or your ancestors?
- What feels eternal in your life right now?

Day 4

- How do the stars connect you to nature—or to something beyond yourself?
- What is one belief you hold that feels grounded in the cosmos, not chaos?
- How would your day be different if you remembered the night sky more often?

Day 5

- What illusions or distractions did the stars help dissolve tonight?
- Which thoughts seemed smaller under the vastness of the sky?
- What brings you peace when you're overwhelmed by the immensity of life?

Day 6

- Did you feel more like a spectator or participant in the cosmos tonight?
- What helps you hold both your smallness and sacredness at once?
- What would it mean to live in rhythm with something greater?

Day 7

- How has stargazing affected your inner world this week?
- What parts of yourself feel reconnected, reoriented, or realigned?
- What personal ritual could you create to carry this sacred practice forward?

Awaken

47
COMPASSION LETTER (INSPIRED BY BUDDHIST AND PSYCHOLOGICAL PRACTICES)

Compassion is that which makes the heart tremble when others suffer.

— THE BUDDHA

Compassion is a bridge between the self and others, between pain and peace, between wounding and healing. In Buddhist teachings, compassion (*karuṇā*) is not merely a feeling but a disciplined practice of seeing suffering clearly and responding with wisdom. In modern psychology, compassion-focused writing has been shown to reduce shame, ease anxiety, and build empathy.[*]

In Buddhist psychology, cultivating compassion involves recognizing the suffering of self and others without clinging to blame or resentment.[†] Teachers like Thích Nhất Hạnh often encourage writing letters to speak honestly from the heart, grounded in awareness and forgiveness.

---

[*] Kristin Neff and Christopher Germer, *The Mindful Self-Compassion Workbook* (New York: Guilford Press, 2018), 131–136.
[†] Thích Nhất Hạnh, *Teachings on Love*, rev. ed. (Berkeley: Parallax Press, 2007), 89–96.

Modern psychology echoes. Studies in compassion-focused therapy and expressive writing show that writing letters to those involved in unresolved emotional experiences can reduce physiological stress, foster empathy, and increase emotional clarity.* Whether or not the letter is ever sent, the act of writing itself can restore a sense of agency, healing, and connection.

Weekly Practice: Compassion Letter

This week, you are invited to write a compassion letter to someone you've hurt, or someone who has hurt you. You may choose to send it or not. The healing happens in the writing: in telling the truth, softening judgment, and offering understanding where there was once pain.

INSTRUCTIONS:

1. Choose someone to whom you want to extend compassion —yourself included.
2. Write them a letter. Be honest. Acknowledge pain. Speak from the heart.
3. Include these three phrases in your own words:
    ○ *This is what hurt.*
    ○ *This is what I've learned or see differently now.*
    ○ *This is what I wish for you (or for us) moving forward.*
4. Read the letter aloud to yourself or place it in a meaningful space.
5. You may burn, bury, keep, or send it—trust what feels right.

Compassion does not always mean reconciliation. But it does

---

* James W. Pennebaker and Joshua M. Smyth, *Opening Up by Writing It Down*, 3rd ed. (New York: Guilford Press, 2016), 67–72.

mean releasing the grip of resentment. This week may your words become a balm for your own heart, and perhaps for someone else's. Let your letter reflect your courage to feel, forgive, and start anew.

Reflection Journal

Day 1

- Who comes to mind when you think of unfinished pain or forgiveness?
- What holds you back from addressing this relationship or memory?
- How might compassion serve both you and them?

Day 2

- What does it feel like to begin writing honestly about hurt?
- Where do you feel resistance—and where do you feel release?
- What do you need to say that you've never said before?

Day 3

- What surprised you in writing this letter—about yourself, or the other person?
- What part of your story feels different now that it's written out?
- What have you learned about pain and perspective?

Day 4

- If you chose not to send the letter, why? What does that mean to you?
- If you did send it, what intention did you carry?
- What does letting go mean in the context of this relationship?

_____
_____
_____
_____
_____
_____
_____
_____

Day 5

- How has your understanding of compassion evolved this week?
- What would it look like to extend that same compassion to yourself?
- Where do you still feel tangled, and where do you feel clearer?

_____
_____
_____
_____
_____

Day 6

- Revisit your letter. What feels true, and what feels tender?
- What would you write differently today, if anything?
- How does this practice impact your understanding of justice and mercy?

Day 7

- Reflect on your emotional and spiritual state before and after writing the letter.
- What does compassion require of you—and what does it give back?
- What commitment do you want to carry forward after this week?

48
SPIRITUAL BATHING (INSPIRED BY YORUBA, JEWISH, AND INDIGENOUS TRADITIONS)

Water knows how to hold, how to release, and how to begin again.

— *GLOBAL WATER TEACHINGS*

Across many cultures, water is not only physical; it is spiritual. It cleanses more than the body; it renews the spirit. In Yoruba tradition, ritual baths called *omi ero* are used for healing, protection, and spiritual attunement. In Judaism, the mikveh is a sacred immersion, a rite of purification and transformation. Indigenous ceremonies around the world, from sweat lodges to river immersions, honor water as a teacher and ally.[*]

In Yoruba cosmology, ritual bathing is a common practice for spiritual cleansing, often performed with herbs, prayers, or guidance from an *òrìṣà* (divine spirit). The bath is not symbolic; it is believed to wash away spiritual heaviness, restore clarity, and realign the inner world.[†]

---

[*] Erika Buenaflor, *Cleanse Your Body, Reveal Your Soul: Indigenous Shamanic Cleansing Rituals for Physical and Spiritual Healing* (Rochester, VT: Bear & Company, 2018), 55–60.
[†] Afolabi A. Epega and Philip Neimark, *The Sacred Ifa Oracle* (San Francisco: HarperOne, 1995), 92–94.

The Jewish *mikveh* is a practice of immersion used not only for purification but also for spiritual transition, such as before weddings, after childbirth, during mourning, or upon conversion. It honors liminal moments: when something old has come to an end and something new begins.*

Among Indigenous peoples, water is a sacred relative. In many traditions, bathing in rivers or lakes is performed with prayers, songs, or plant medicine, and is considered a way to reconnect with the land, ancestors, and one's own spiritual strength.†

Weekly Practice: Spiritual Bathing

This week, you are invited to turn your bath or shower into a sacred ritual. With salt, herbs, or simple presence, bless your body. Release what you no longer need. Invite renewal.

INSTRUCTIONS:

1. Prepare a bath or foot soak (or shower, if preferred). Add salt, herbs, flowers, or essential oils.
2. Light a candle or speak a blessing aloud.
3. As you enter the water, say: *"May all that is heavy be released. May all that is sacred be restored."*
4. Gently wash your body. Pause and breathe deeply.
5. When finished, give thanks to the water and let it carry away what no longer serves.

Spiritual bathing is a ritual of remembering: your body is sacred, your energy is valuable, and your spirit can be renewed. Let this week's waters hold you, cleanse you, and return you to yourself.

---

* Rachel Adler, *Engendering Judaism: An Inclusive Theology and Ethics* (Philadelphia: Jewish Publication Society, 1998), 170–175.
† Robin Wall Kimmerer, *Braiding Sweetgrass: Indigenous Wisdom, Scientific Knowledge, and the Teachings of Plants*(Minneapolis: Milkweed Editions, 2013), 301–307.

Reflection Journal

Day 1

- How do you usually approach bathing—routine or ritual?
- What intentions would you like to bring into your next bath or shower?
- What do you long to wash away?

_____
_____
_____
_____
_____
_____
_____
_____

Day 2

- How did it feel to bless your body with water today?
- What emotions surfaced during or after the practice?
- What part of your body needs the most tenderness right now?

_____
_____
_____
_____

Day 3

- What herbs, scents, or symbols feel spiritually significant to you?
- How can you customize your bathing ritual to reflect your path or heritage?
- What does sacred self-care mean to you?

Day 4

- What energy are you releasing, and what are you making space for?
- How do you want to feel when you step out of the water?
- What kind of prayers or affirmations feel authentic for your journey?

Day 5

- What does water teach you about boundaries, flow, or surrender?
- How can you carry the softness of the bath into the rest of your day?
- Where do you feel most cleansed—physically, emotionally, spiritually?

Day 6

- What ancestral or cultural connections might you explore through water rituals?
- How does your inner world respond when your outer body is honored?
- What rhythms or cycles in your life call for this kind of renewal?

_____
_____
_____
_____
_____
_____
_____
_____

Day 7

- Reflect on this week's spiritual bathing practice—what has shifted?
- How might you make this a regular ritual of reset and blessing?
- What does your body now know that your mind had forgotten?

_____
_____
_____
_____

Awaken

49

PRACTICE OF STILLNESS (INSPIRED BY THE YOGIC TRADITION)

Yoga is the journey of the self, through the self, to the Self.

— BHAGAVAD GĪTĀ

In the ancient teachings of yoga, stillness is the presence of being. Beyond physical postures (*asanas*) lies a deeper aim: inner peace through the mastery of attention. Patanjali's Yoga Sutras define yoga as the "stilling of the fluctuations of the mind."[*] When we learn to sit in silence, we awaken to something larger than thought, we awaken to the awareness itself.

THE CLASSICAL EIGHTFOLD path of yoga (*ashtanga yoga*) culminates in meditation and stillness: *dhyāna* (contemplation) and *samādhi* (spiritual absorption).[†] In yogic philosophy, stillness is not separate from movement but the source beneath it. Even when the body is active,

---

[*] Patanjali, *The Yoga Sutras of Patanjali*, trans. Sri Swami Satchidananda (Yogaville, VA: Integral Yoga Publications, 2012), Sutra 1.2.
[†] Georg Feuerstein, *The Yoga Tradition: Its History, Literature, Philosophy and Practice* (Prescott, AZ: Hohm Press, 2008), 253–259.

the goal is to maintain inner steadiness—a state known as *sthira sukham asanam*, "the posture is steady and easeful."*

While much of modern yoga emphasizes movement, traditional yogis practiced long periods of seated stillness, often outdoors, eyes soft or closed, breathing gently. Stillness becomes a sacred container where the ego softens, clarity arises, and the boundaries between self and source dissolve.

Weekly Practice: Stillness

This week, your practice is to simply sit. No striving. No perfect posture required. Just you, your breath, and the quiet presence underneath it all.

INSTRUCTIONS:

1. Choose a quiet place. Sit comfortably with a straight spine —on the floor, chair, or cushion.
2. Set a timer for 10–20 minutes. Close your eyes or gaze softly ahead.
3. Focus on your breath or a simple inward mantra (e.g., *So Hum*, meaning "I am That").
4. When thoughts come, gently return to the breath or stillness.
5. End with a bow, hand to heart, or whispered word of thanks.

Stillness is not an escape from the world. It is a return to what is real beneath the noise. Let your practice this week remind you that you are not your thoughts, you are the witness. The peace you seek is already within.

---

* T. K. V. Desikachar, *The Heart of Yoga: Developing a Personal Practice* (Rochester, VT: Inner Traditions, 1995), 17.

Reflection Journal

Day 1

- What is your current relationship with stillness—avoidance, longing, resistance?
- How did your body respond to sitting quietly today?
- What thoughts were hardest to release? Which were easiest?

_____
_____
_____
_____
_____
_____
_____
_____

Day 2

- What distractions pulled at your attention during stillness?
- How did you bring yourself back without judgment?
- What did you notice beneath the surface of silence?

_____
_____
_____
_____
_____

Day 3

- What sensations, images, or memories arose in the stillness today?
- What would it mean to allow rather than control your inner experience?
- What part of you feels more spacious or calm after this practice?

Day 4

- What is being revealed to you through this stillness?
- How does your breath guide your return to presence?
- What helps you soften rather than strive?

Day 5

- Has anything shifted in your nervous system or emotional state since beginning this practice?
- How might stillness support your spiritual growth or healing?
- What false urgency in your life are you ready to release?

Day 6

- What is the difference between stillness and stagnation—for you?
- How has your inner dialogue changed over the course of the week?
- What does your soul say in the quiet?

_____
_____
_____
_____
_____
_____
_____
_____

Day 7

- Reflect on your week of stillness. What have you learned about yourself?
- What moments of grace or insight emerged from simply sitting?
- How might you protect time for stillness in your ongoing spiritual rhythm?

_____
_____
_____
_____

50

SEASONAL GRATITUDE OFFERING (INSPIRED BY THE KALASHA PEOPLE OF THE HINDU KUSH)

The season is alive. Greet it with joy, or it may turn away.

— KALASHA PROVERB

High in the valleys of the Hindu Kush mountains live the Kalasha, a small Indigenous community known for their vibrant festivals, animist spirituality, and devotion to sacred joy. For the Kalasha, life is centered around the natural seasons, the mountain spirits, and the idea that gratitude is not just a feeling; it's a form of balance. Each season is welcomed with offerings, dances, prayers, and songs.*

The Kalasha follows a spiritual calendar marked by major seasonal festivals: *Joshi* (spring), *Uchau* (autumn), *Pul* (harvest), and *Chaumos* (winter solstice). These are not merely cultural events. They are sacred rituals to express gratitude to the deities of nature, fertility, and time. Offerings may include milk, fruit, flowers, or symbolic

---

* Wynne R. Maggi, *Our Women Are Free: Gender and Ethnicity in the Hindukush* (Ann Arbor: University of Michigan Press, 2001), 42–46.

objects, placed near shrines or natural features. Joy, laughter, and color are seen as signs of spiritual alignment.*

The Kalasha do not worship in silence or austerity, but in celebration. Their worldview reminds us that spiritual gratitude doesn't always need to be solemn; it can be as simple as dancing, laughing, or offering a handful of berries to the earth with a smile. Even small rituals, when done with intention, restore harmony between humans and the sacred world.

Weekly Practice: Gratitude Offering

This week, you are invited into the Kalasha-inspired practice of seasonal gratitude. Tune into the season you are in (whether literal or symbolic) and offer thanks to the unseen forces that nourish your life. Offer with joy. Offer with presence. Offer with your whole being.

INSTRUCTIONS:

1. Step outside and take a moment to observe the season around you.
2. Gather a symbolic offering—a flower, stone, fruit, or breath of thanks.
3. Place it in nature or a sacred space with this simple blessing:
    - *"I offer this to the spirit of this season, in gratitude for life."*
4. Optional: add music, movement, or laughter as part of the ritual.
5. Repeat daily, tuning into different aspects of the season and your emotional state.

The Kalasha teaches us that gratitude is not just a private

---

* Peter Parkes, "Kalasha Environmental Cosmology and the Sacred Value of Milk," *Anthropology Today* 7, no. 4 (1991): 3–10.

thought; it's a public celebration of the sacred. This week, let the turning of the season remind you that joy is a worthy form of devotion. You are part of nature's dance. Don't forget to say thank you.

Reflection Journal

Day 1

- What season are you in—literally, emotionally, or spiritually?
- How has this season shaped your thoughts, energy, or patterns?
- What feels ripe for gratitude today?

_____
_____
_____
_____
_____
_____
_____
_____

Day 2

- What does it mean to honor the season rather than resist it?
- How might you align your actions more closely with the rhythms of nature?

- What would it look like to give thanks for what's *still becoming*?

- Day 3
- What small joy today felt sacred or surprising?
- How can celebration itself be a spiritual act?
- What would it mean to express gratitude with your body —not just your words?

Day 4

- What would you offer the earth today as a symbol of appreciation?
- How does this act shift your awareness of the world around you?
- What's one tradition you could create to mark seasonal transitions?

Day 5

- What role does beauty or color play in your spirituality?
- How might you bring more playfulness into your devotional life?
- What joy have you withheld from yourself that is ready to return?

Day 6

- How has the practice of seasonal offering shifted your inner pace or mindset?
- What are you now noticing in your environment that you missed before?
- What does gratitude look like when you *feel* it, not just think it?

Day 7

- Reflect on your week of seasonal gratitude. What deepened or changed?
- What will you carry forward from this practice into the next season?
- How might you embody the Kalasha wisdom: joy as harmony, gratitude as devotion?

51

REMEMBERING THE ANCESTORS (INSPIRED BY JAPANESE SHINTO AND BUDDHIST TRADITIONS)

To forget one's ancestors is to be a river without a source, a tree without roots.

— *JAPANESE PROVERB*

In Japanese tradition, remembering one's ancestors is not just a ritual. It is a way of life. Ancestors are considered part of the living household, present in spirit, and worthy of daily respect. The practice of *sosen suhai* (ancestor veneration) blends Shinto reverence for the spirits (*kami*) with Buddhist memorial rites, reminding us that we live because others have lived, sacrificed, and loved.[*] Each year during *Obon*, Japanese families return home, light lanterns, and welcome the spirits of the ancestors. But this remembering doesn't need to wait for a festival. It can happen every day with a candle, a whisper, a name.

In Shinto, it is believed that the spirits of ancestors become *kami*, revered presences who protect and guide the living. Many homes have a *kamidana* (Shinto altar) or a *butsudan* (Buddhist altar), where

---

[*] Robert S. Ellwood, *Introducing Japanese Religion* (New York: Routledge, 2007), 125–128.

offerings of incense, rice, and prayers are made to departed loved ones.* This practice is not about mourning, but connection. The dead are not "gone"; they continue to exist in relationship with the living.

During *Obon*, a summer festival rooted in both Shinto and Buddhist beliefs, families' light fires and lanterns to guide the ancestors' spirits home and later send them off again with prayers of gratitude. These acts of remembrance are not based on dogma but on devotion. It is an invitation to live with awareness that we are never alone.†

Weekly Practice: Remembering Our Ancestors

This week, we pause to remember our ancestors who have gone before us and giving honor to them.

Instructions:

1. Choose a quiet moment. Light a candle or incense.
2. Speak aloud the names of your ancestors or say:
   - *"I remember those who came before me. I honor your life and your spirit."*
3. Place a photo, memento, or cup of tea near the candle if you wish.
4. Offer a short prayer, bow, or moment of silence.
5. Repeat daily. Let it be simple, sincere, and from the heart.

To remember our ancestors is to return to our roots. In honoring those who came before us, we honor ourselves, not out of obligation, but because remembrance is an act of love. May this week deepen your sense of belonging to a lineage greater than yourself.

---

* Ian Reader, *Religion in Contemporary Japan* (Honolulu: University of Hawai'i Press, 1991), 71–75.
† Helen Hardacre, *Shinto: A History* (New York: Oxford University Press, 2017), 454–459.

Reflection Journal

Day 1

- Who in your family line do you think of most often?
- What stories have been passed down—and what has been forgotten?
- How does it feel to say their name aloud today?

_____
_____
_____
_____
_____
_____
_____
_____

Day 2

- What did your ancestors live through that shaped your life today?
- How might your life be a continuation—or transformation—of their legacy?
- What wisdom or strength do you inherit from them?

_____
_____
_____

Day 3

- What simple offering feels appropriate today—a memory, food, a word of thanks?
- What role does reverence play in your spirituality?
- How might this practice reconnect you with something sacred?

Day 4

- If you could ask one ancestor a question, what would it be?
- What do you wish to say to them that's never been said?
- What emotions arise when you imagine them nearby?

Day 5.

- What rituals of remembrance did your parents or grandparents practice?
- How do cultural or religious traditions shape how you think about death and legacy?
- What rituals do you want to create or pass on?

Day 6

- How has this practice changed your awareness of your roots?
- What burdens or patterns do you feel called to heal in your lineage?
- What blessings are you noticing?

_____
_____
_____
_____
_____
_____
_____
_____

Day 7

- Reflect on this week. What did you learn about your connection to the past?
- What presence did you feel in the quiet moments?
- How will you continue honoring your ancestors in everyday life?

_____
_____
_____
_____
_____
_____

52

BUILDING YOUR OWN RITUAL (INSPIRED BY THE GLOBAL TAPESTRY OF PRACTICE)

Your daily life is your temple and your religion.

— *KHALIL GIBRAN*

You have traveled through 51 weeks of spiritual practice; walking with sages, ancestors, and seekers from many lands. You've sat in stillness, danced with joy, gazed at stars, honored the earth, and listened to your own soul. Now, you are invited to do something profoundly sacred: create a ritual that is uniquely yours.

Ritual is not reserved for priests or monks. It is for anyone who chooses to live intentionally. A ritual can be grand or simple, ancient or improvised. It is born where meaning and mindfulness meet. And it begins with this question: *What helps you remember who you are?*

Across traditions, ritual has served as a vessel for the sacred, a way to embody values, mark time, heal wounds, and remember what matters. In Indigenous cultures, rituals arise from the land and evolve with the people. In Hindu and Buddhist systems, daily offerings and breath-centered rituals train the mind toward awareness. In modern spiritual psychology, even small personal rituals (such as lighting a candle, journaling, or repeating a mantra) are linked to increased resilience, emotional balance, and a sense of purpose.*

You don't need to follow a formula. You need only to listen: What nourished you most this year? What brought you peace, clarity, or strength? Let your ritual be a blend of those elements and be a mirror of your spirit.

Weekly Practice: Create Your Own Ritual

Take time this week to design a simple spiritual ritual for yourself. Choose a few elements from past weeks that resonated deeply—stillness, movement, nature, prayer, sound, breath, offerings, reflection. Combine them into a 5–15-minute practice that you can return to regularly. Give your ritual a name or phrase. Write it down. Make it yours. Try it once each day this week, adjusting it as needed to fit your life.

This is not the end; it's a beginning. You now carry a treasury of practices that span centuries and continents. Use them not to perform, but to stay awake. Let your ritual become a quiet revolution: a way of choosing presence in a world of distraction, and peace in a world of noise.

Reflection Journal

Day 1

- What practices from this year have felt most meaningful or nourishing?
- What do you want your personal ritual to help you remember each day?
- What spiritual needs are you hoping this ritual will meet?

---

* Casper ter Kuile, *The Power of Ritual: Turning Everyday Activities into Soulful Practices* (New York: HarperOne, 2020), 32–38.

Day 2

- What elements feel essential to your ritual—movement, silence, words, symbols?
- What time of day or place will support this practice most naturally?
- How will you begin and end your ritual?

Day 3

- Try your new ritual today. What flowed easily? What felt awkward or unclear?
- How did your body, breath, or energy shift during or after the practice?
- What surprised you about the experience?

_____
_____
_____
_____
_____
_____
_____
_____
_____

Day 4

- What does it mean to you to "own" your spirituality?
- How can your ritual reflect both your personal truth and collective wisdom?
- What would it look like to pass this practice on to others?

_____
_____
_____
_____
_____
_____
_____
_____
_____

Day 5

- How does creating your own ritual challenge old ideas of religion or identity?
- What stories or beliefs do you want your ritual to embody or release?
- What would it mean to live a life that is itself a ritual?

_____
_____
_____
_____
_____
_____
_____
_____

Day 6

- Repeat your ritual. What needs refining, simplifying, or strengthening?
- How might this practice evolve over time or with the seasons?
- What role will this ritual play in your resilience moving forward?

_____
_____
_____
_____
_____

Day 7

- Reflect on your spiritual journey over the past 52 weeks. What has changed?
- What do you now know—deeply and truly—that you didn't know before?
- How will you carry this work, and this wisdom, into the rest of your life?

CONCLUSION: AWAKEN AGAIN— AND KEEP BECOMING

You have walked through many doors. Some you recognized. Some were waiting to be remembered. Now you carry them inside you.

Over these 52 weeks, you've stepped into the sacred rhythm of resilience—one breath, one practice, one awakening at a time. You've touched ancient wisdom. You've honored silence and joy. You've come home to yourself. But this is not the end. This is your beginning. As your journey deepens, so will ours. There are still sacred conversations waiting to be had. About love and embodiment. About healing and identity. About spirit, story, justice, relationship, and freedom.

Let gratitude anchor you. And when you're ready—Awaken again. And again. Because the journey is sacred. And so are you.

ACKNOWLEDGMENTS

This book is more than a guide—it's a witness. Born from seasons of spiritual fire and gentle healing, *Awaken* is the result of not only study and service, but surrender.

To my family—thank you for loving me through the intensity of creation. Your presence grounded me when I felt lost in the process.

To Micheal, Kim, Sam, Crystal, Shelby, and Sara—thank you for standing by me, listening when I needed it most, and reminding me who I am—especially when I forgot.

To Matt—thank you for your steady presence and for the Bible—both of which I desperately needed during one of the hardest times in my life.

To the many mentors, teachers, and wisdom-keepers who have shaped my understanding of spirit, resilience, and sacred rhythm, I offer my deepest gratitude.

I have done my best to honor and respect the traditions from which each practice in this book is drawn. Where adaptation was necessary, it was done with reverence, not appropriation. I recognize the sacred roots of these practices and remain a student of their depth.

I also want to acknowledge the role of Grammarly and ChatGPT-4o, which I used as editorial tools throughout this project. These AI-assisted platforms helped strengthen the grammar, structure, and clarity of the text. However, all responsibility for the content, direction, and spirit of this work remains entirely my own.

This book is not perfect—and neither am I. If there are errors, omissions, or areas where I've fallen short, I receive that feedback with humility. I own those mistakes and remain committed to learning.

And finally, to you—the reader, the seeker, the soul-sore and soul-strong—I see you. May this book be a companion on your journey home to the sacred center within.

ABOUT THE AUTHOR

Adam R. Boggess is a spiritual resilience educator, life coach, and founder of Tatted Chaps Press. A former U.S. Marine turned interfaith leader, he now serves as a Navy Chaplain, offering over two decades of military service and soul-centered guidance to individuals, families, and communities navigating life's most demanding seasons.

Currently based in Okinawa, Japan, Adam leads personal resilience retreats that focus on helping participants recover hope, reclaim their purpose, and rebuild inner strength. His approach combines evidence-informed strategies with ancient wisdom, promoting holistic healing that encompasses the mind, body, and spirit.

Adam holds advanced degrees in theology and pastoral counseling and is pursuing a Ph.D. in Mind-Body Medicine. His interdisciplinary work integrates global religious traditions, psychology, metaphysics, and lived experience. He is especially committed to making spiritual growth accessible, inclusive, and transformative for those experiencing grief, transition, or soul fatigue.

Outside of his professional work, Adam finds joy riding his motorcycle along coastal roads, playing traditional Okinawan music on the sanshin, and sharing meaningful conversations over tea. Above all, he treasures time with his family—his deepest source of purpose, love, and grounding.

www.ingramcontent.com/pod-product-compliance
Lightning Source LLC
LaVergne TN
LVHW091246080426
835510LV00007B/140